Peace & Joy
To GAIL

Knowing and Loving

The Keys to Real Happiness

By

Robert Beezat

First published by Dog Ear Publishing
4010 W. 86th Street, Ste H
Indianapolis, IN 46268
www.dogearpublishing.net

ISBN: 978-160844-606-3

This book is printed on acid-free paper.

Printed in the United States of America

TABLE OF CONTENTS

Chapter One:

Knowing and Loving..Page 1

Chapter Two:

Knowledge and Belief..Page 5

Chapter Three:

Types of Knowledge ....Page 10

Chapter Four:

Love, Knowledge, and Belief..............................Page 14

Chapter Five:

The Most Basic Question: Why is There Something

Instead of Nothing? ....Page 18

Chapter Six:

Limits to and History of Talking About God ....Page 23

Chapter Seven:

What I Think About God.......................................Page 28

Chapter Eight:

Change, Evolution, and God ....Page 32

Chapter Nine:

What and Who Am I?...Page 38

Chapter Ten:

Why Am I Here?...Page 45

Chapter Eleven:

What is Happiness? ....Page 53

Chapter Twelve:

What Does Knowledge Have to Do With Happiness? ....Page 59

Chapter Thirteen:

The Pursuit of Happiness ....Page 63

Chapter Fourteen:

Truth, Goodness, and Beauty Defined ....Page 69

Chapter Fifteen:

Truth, Goodness, and Beauty in Relationship

to Happiness ....Page 77

Chapter Sixteen:

Evil ....Page 81

Chapter Seventeen:

Happiness and the God Factor..Page 93

Chapter Eighteen:

Religion, Spirituality, and Happiness...............................Page 98

Chapter Nineteen:

Why I Am a Catholic..Page 102

Chapter Twenty:

Praying For Wisdom, Strength, and Courage ....Page 108

Chapter Twenty-One:

Work ....Page 112

Chapter Twenty-Two:

What is Marriage? ....Page 127

Chapter Twenty-Three:

Why Get Married Today? ....Page 131

Chapter Twenty-Four:

Why Do So Many Marriages Fail?...................................Page 136

Chapter Twenty-Five:

Raising Children...Page 148

Chapter Twenty-Six:

    Have Fun! ....Page 159

Chapter Twenty-Seven:

    Uncertainty..Page 165

Chapter Twenty-Eight:

    Summary and Conclusion ....Page 177

CHAPTER ONE

Knowing and Loving

We are born to know and love.

That is what makes us distinctly human beings.

We are born to do other things as well. We can and should "eat, drink, and be merry." Pleasure is an important part of being a human being. Most of us need to work. Most of us need to perform many mundane tasks which require our time and energy in order to survive and function in the world in which we live.

But what makes us human and distinguishes us from all other beings and entities that we are aware of are our unique capacities and ways of knowing and loving. And it is those unique capacities to know and love which make us truly happy as human beings.

In order to live happy lives, we need to understand who and what we are as human beings. We need to know what it really means to be a being which is capable of knowing and loving. We need to know how we fit into the broader realities with which we interact in every facet of our lives.

Who Am I? What Am I? Why Am I Here? Is there a God? What will really make me happy?

These are some of the questions we all ask ourselves from time to time. Our answers to, or avoidance of, those questions shape the choices we make which, in turn, determine our depth of happiness.

Living a happy life and a good life requires us to have as clear an understanding of reality as possible. The better understanding we have of reality as it truly is, not as we are told it is or hope it is, then the better chance we have of making decisions and choices that will help us to build and live a good life…a happy life… a life full of loving relationships.

"Ideas have consequences" is a quote that I heard or read many years ago. It is a statement that I think is very true. What we know and think has a large impact on how we act as individuals and as a society.

The purpose of this book is twofold:

1.   To try to come as close as possible to understanding who and what we are as human beings, as well as the realities outside of ourselves with which we interact; and,
2.   Based on that knowledge and understanding, to make decisions and choices which will help us flourish as human beings.

The following essays (*attempts*, as the root word of essay means) try to address a broad range of questions which start at the very beginning of what it means to exist and then to translate those basic understandings into practical applications which can help us lead happy, full and good lives filled with loving relationships.

I don't say that my answers will be, or have to be, accepted by everyone. I know very well that I see the world through my lens of knowledge and experience. But I have been a lifelong learner. I have read hundreds of books and thousands of articles on a broad range of topics, including, but not limited to: art, history, science, philosophy, literature, business, economics, politics, theology, culture, etc. I have listened to and conversed with many knowledgeable and good people. I have worked diligently and consistently over a lifetime to understand all of reality as best I can.

I have written this book because I think my ideas may be helpful to others who are trying to think about and then live a good and full human life. In the following pages, I am going to start at the beginning, ask some very basic questions, and tell you what I have learned. I think all of us ponder these basic questions from time to time. I think the answers to these questions determine how we relate to and interact with reality; and, in turn, how happy a life we enjoy.

The first chapters of the book raise and attempt to answer some very basic questions. The chapters in the latter part of this book attempt to relate these broad and deep concepts to some of our everyday encounters with reality inside and outside of ourselves. And as part of the discussion of those ideas, I will talk about how those ideas can be translated into building a happy and good life for ourselves and those around us.

My suggestion to readers is that you move through this book slowly. Read a chapter or two at a time. Take a few days to think about the ideas you have encountered in the chapter. Think about how you live your life and what experiences you've had which either agree or disagree with the thoughts in the particular chapter.

My intention is to provoke your thoughts about who and what you are and the experiences that have brought you to where you are today. Your answers may be different than mine in major or minor ways. That is fine. None of us has a grasp on the whole truth of reality. We don't have to all come up with the same answers. The important thing is to think about and know reality as clearly as we are able to do, and then act accordingly.

It is never too late to start living a life which emphasizes under-standing reality as it truly is and then making choices and decisions in response to that reality. Whenever we begin to do so, we will have a better chance to be happier and to start or improve our loving rela-tionships with others. I hope this book helps you along that path.

CHAPTER TWO

Knowledge and Belief

All of us think we know many things. In fact, most of the time, we only know parts of things or the probabilities of things.

All of us think that we only believe in a few things (like God or the Easter Bunny) or think we believe in nothing at all. In fact, most of what we think we know are really things that we believe.

There are only a few things that we know absolutely and completely. For instance, *I know* that I am sitting at a computer and typing this sentence right now. *I know* that my fingers are hitting the keys. To me, both of those sentences are absolutely and completely true. My knowledge as contained in both of those sentences cannot be contradicted or are not a figment of my imagination.

To a lesser degree, I know that my brain is sending electronic messages to my fingers to do this typing. I don't know that with the same certainty with which I know I am sitting in front of this computer and typing. The reason I do not know that with the same certainty I exist is that I cannot feel, see or smell, or in any way sense, that electronic messages are coursing through my nervous system from my brain to my fingers. However, I have read articles about electronic messages from the brain to various body parts, so I think that is what is happening.

On the other hand, I *believe* that I will be sitting at this computer again within the next few days doing some additional writing. I do not *know* that I will be at this computer in a few days, but the probabilities are pretty high.

There are many ways to think about knowledge and belief. I find it helpful to look at both ideas on a continuum as follows:

Continuum of Knowledge

```
Minimal                                              Complete
Knowledge__/_____/_____/_____/___Knowledge
       Nematodes      Wine         Cities      I exist
```

In terms of the continuum of knowledge, we all know different things at different points on the continuum. On the minimal side, I know practically nothing about nematodes.   I know a little bit about wine. Since my career has been in city government for 35 years, I know a lot about cities. Finally, I have complete knowledge that I exist.

My knowledge is based on my experience and learning. I know that I exist. I know that from my own experience. I did not have to learn that anywhere from anyone. On the other hand, what I know about pretty much anything else can be anywhere along the continuum of knowledge. If, for example, I always existed in a room without light, sound, or any other sensory stimulation, my knowledge of reality would be very limited. It would be far to the left of the continuum. If I lived in an environment where I was well-educated and had the opportunity to learn many things in both academic and practical spheres, my knowledge overall would be to the right side of the continuum, but it could be anywhere along the continuum, depending on the topic.

Continuum of Belief

```
Less Credible                                      More Credible
Belief_____/_____/_____/_____Belief
        The Martians    I will live at      Belief    Sun will rise
        are coming!     least 5 more years  in God    tomorrow
```

In terms of the continuum of belief, we all believe different things at different points on the continuum. Beliefs are either more credible or less credible. The credibility of our belief depends primarily on three things: knowledge, experience, and credibility of the source. For instance, there is no need for belief as far as my own existence is concerned. I *know* that I exist. I experience that. No one needs to tell me that. And, unless I am mentally ill in some way or other, I am credible to myself regarding the matter of my existence.

An example of a very credible belief is the matter of whether the sun will rise tomorrow. All of my learning and all of my experience tells me that this is almost an absolute certainty. Every trained physicist will give me many reasons why it will do so tomorrow. But it is possible that the sun will not rise tomorrow because maybe earth will be hit by a large asteroid during the night and will exist no more. The sun will be rising somewhere, but it won't be on earth.

When I consider whether I will live five more years, my belief is less certain and less credible than whether or not the sun will come out tomorrow. I have knowledge of my health, my age, the way I live my life, etc. The chances are that I will be alive five years from now, but it is not a certainty. My belief might be increased somewhat if an actuary showed me statistics which indicated that, more than likely I will be alive in five years. Probabilities play a role in belief. Also, my belief might be increased somewhat if I'd just had my physical, and the doctor told me I was in great shape. But in the final analysis, I believe that I will live for five more years. I don't know that.

The statement that "The Martians are coming!" is a very low level credible belief. It is possible, but not very likely. Our knowledge of Mars indicates there is not life on the planet. Our experience of extra-terrestrial life is non-existent. And the only ones who might think the statement is true are those who have been taken up on

UFO's and then dropped off in Roswell, New Mexico. Is it possible that there are Martians and they are coming? I suppose the answer is "Yes," but it is not likely or credible.

Somewhere along that continuum of belief is a belief in God. For myself, I would place that belief somewhere on the continuum between my belief that the sun will rise tomorrow and that I will live five more years. As I will discuss in subsequent chapters, there are several reasons why I think that some type of God exists is a credible belief. That choice is based on my knowledge and experience. It is also based on the credible witness and thoughts of generations of extremely intelligent and thoughtful people.

Knowledge and belief are not two separate and mutually exclusive domains. They overlap and complement each other. Seldom do we know anything absolutely and totally, and seldom do we believe anything absolutely and totally.

Generally, the more we know and the higher the credibility of our beliefs, the closer we are to understanding reality. The contrary is also true: the less we know and the less credible our beliefs, the farther away we are from understanding reality.

It is important to understand reality, because we do not live in a vacuum. We need to act. We try to act in accordance with our best knowledge and/or with our most credible beliefs.

The less knowledge we have and the less credible our beliefs, the more likely it is that we will make bad decisions and take inappropriate actions. The better our knowledge and the more credible our beliefs, the more likely it is that we will make good decisions and take appropriate actions, which help us live good human lives and help others do the same.

I plan my life and take actions based on the strong belief that the sun will come up tomorrow. I also plan my life and take actions on the belief that I will be alive for the next five years. Of course, I am not certain of that. I pursue my city government career based on my extensive knowledge of that field. Since I am a consultant to cities, I try to continue to increase my knowledge in this field because it will make me a more credible "expert" to my clients if I am current in my field. In fact, what I sell mainly to my clients is credibility…"I know what I am doing and I will get it done."

Basically, our entire life revolves around actions that we take based on the relative combination of knowledge and belief we bring to every decision or choice we make.

We ask questions.

We seek answers.

We make decisions.

Our mixture of knowledge and belief guides our decisions and our actions. And, it is almost always a combination of the two elements.

Seldom do we, or can we, have perfect, total and complete knowledge. Consequently, our beliefs play a very important role in who we are and how we act.

CHAPTER THREE

Types of Knowledge

There are basically two types of knowledge. They are difficult to define absolutely, but describing what and how we know things can give us some indication of the difference between the two. I should also say that they are not mutually exclusive as types of knowledge. There is a lot of overlap between the two. We usually can't have one type of knowledge without some elements of the other type.

I divide the two types of knowledge into two broad categories:

- Scientific Knowledge
- Experiential Knowledge

Scientific knowledge has several key elements. It is usually reductionist in nature. It starts with the whole and breaks down an entity to its smallest constituent pieces or elements. Scientific knowledge is measurable and reproducible. A person should be able to do the same experiment over and over and get the same result. Scientific knowledge is almost always numbers and mathematics based.

Scientific knowledge has exploded in the last several hundred years. The scientific method has rightfully become accepted as a successful way to understand many aspects of reality. Some who see it as the only way of knowing are certain that someday, all of reality will be explained by scientific knowledge and the scientific method. Some of those same people contend that if something cannot be measured and reduced to constituent pieces, it does not exist. They contend that we have just not figured out how to understand it from a scientific standpoint.

Experiential knowledge is a less precise approach to knowledge, but has a broader base of contact with reality. Experiential knowledge results from encounters with the totality of an entity. It is holistic. It experiences the emergent and integrative aspects of reality. Often, experiential knowledge is imaginative and creative in the way it knows things and the way it expresses itself.

Great art, whether visual, musical, poetical or any other mode of expression, captures aspects of reality that most human beings can relate to and understand. It captures deeper aspects of reality that go beyond what scientific knowledge can tell us about something.

Encounters with other persons in particular, put us in contact with a reality which can be measured in some ways, but cannot be measured in their entirety. The word "encounter" in this case is used to describe a personal, open, face-to-face relationship and communication between two people as described by Martin Buber as "I-Thou" relationships. Most of the time we know other things and people as objects outside of ourselves. We see those objects, including other persons, as something or someone external to us. On the other hand, we see ourselves from a subjective standpoint. We see ourselves as being more complex and not entirely knowable by others.

A true encounter with another person occurs when we see the other person as who they truly are. We connect with that reality in the other person that is truly and deeply who they are. In some ways, we become one with that person and that person becomes one with us. We are both changed by the encounter. We don't lose who we are; neither does the other person. Rather, we both become more because we have encountered the other person at the deepest levels of who we and they are.

That type of knowledge is not measurable. It is not quantifiable. It is difficult to describe. But it does exist. And those who have experienced such "I-Thou" relationships know that it exists whether they can explain it or even accurately describe it. Most people get glimpses of that reality when they experience love. But they also get it through great works of art or in the beauty that surrounds us. Such encounters touch us and speak to us at our deepest level of our consciousness and subconsciousness.

Experiential knowledge does not preclude scientific knowledge. In fact, scientific knowledge expands our contact and encounter with reality. But it only offers one perspective, albeit, an important aspect. On the other hand, scientific knowledge does not preclude experiential knowledge. Scientific research and knowledge often are inspired by and become coherent theories through our experiential knowledge and imagination - our ability as human beings to propose and think about things that have not yet been measured or cannot be measured.

It is foolish and presumptuous to say that the only valid knowledge is scientific knowledge. It is just as foolish and presumptuous to say that knowledge gained through experience and genuine encounters with people and things is more important than scientific knowledge. One does not trump the other. All knowledge should work together to help us understand as much as we can about the reality in which we live. Sometimes the two types of knowledge seem to be in conflict. But if both are true representations of a portion of reality, then what we are not seeing is the connection between the two.

That is why I always liked Einstein's description of genius: the ability to see the connections between things that no one has seen before.

There is so much more that human beings will learn about the universe from a scientific standpoint. Sometimes those discoveries will raise serious questions about our knowledge which we have gained from our broad-based life experiences. When those conflicts arise, we can do one of two things: One, hold fast to our own, preferred mode of knowing and dismiss the new knowledge; or Two, look to expand our knowledge to incorporate the new knowledge into a broader world-view.

Reconciling and broadening my knowledge of reality is pretty much what I have been trying to do since I was a kid. It is not something I pursue because it is a sterile, intellectual puzzle. I pursue that knowledge and understanding because I want my actions, choices, and decisions to be based as best I can on what is really out in the world, not on what I have learned in the past and, which consequently, makes me intellectually and psychologically comfortable and safe.

CHAPTER FOUR

Love, Knowledge, and Belief

One of the things that most of us believe in is love.

"Lover's leap" and "leap of faith" are common expressions.

Both love and faith require a "leap,"…a decision to take an action without knowing all of the facts or how it will turn out.

Telling someone that you love them and want to spend the rest of your life with them is truly a leap of faith. It happens millions of times a day across the globe. Sometimes that faith is rewarded. Sometimes it is not. We all have seen many examples of both results. Many people have seen it in their own lives. Someone once said that second marriages are the triumph of hope over experience. It is also a triumph of faith in something that we believe exists and is important to us, and that is love.

We all want to be loved and we all want to love someone.

Almost everyone wants to "fall in love."

But what is love? And, what does love have to do with belief and knowledge?

Many of us know of love because we have experienced it. Generally, someone has loved us at some time in our lives. Maybe it was a parent or both parents. Maybe it was a grandparent. Maybe it was an aunt or uncle…a friend…a spouse…a lover. If we are fortunate, we have been loved by several people.

Love is something we learn about through experience. Love is a

- **Relational connection** between two people that is
- **Mutually open to and accepting** of the other person,

- **Desires and acts for the well-being of the other** person, and has at its core,
- The **desire to be one** with that person.

We know love exists because we have experienced it. We can, to some degree, rationally talk about love. But love is really something we experience. We can describe it to some degree, but we never capture it in words alone. That is why art forms of all kinds do a better job of describing love than rational explanations.

Science can tell us that our heartbeats increase when in the presence of someone we love. It can describe many other physical manifestations of love; whether it is a mother's love for a child, a friend's love for a friend, or a lover's love for a lover. But those descriptions are not a definition of love nor are they the reality of love. Scientific knowledge is inadequate as a method of knowing about and describing love.

Love is a reality. I have experienced it. I think many of us have. I don't think that it is a material reality, though it certainly has physical manifestations. It cannot be defined by, or reduced to, material elements. On the continuum of knowledge talked about in an earlier chapter, the reality of love, to me, is at the right side of the continuum. I am not as certain in my knowledge of the reality of love as I am that I am typing this sentence. I am also not as certain of my knowledge of love as I am that the sun will rise tomorrow. But I have experienced love enough over my lifetime to know that it exists. I also believe in love in the sense that I will continue to experience it. On the continuum of belief, it is a very credible belief that I will continue to love and be loved.

I think it is important to say that our experience of love can be divided into two kinds of events. One is the actual experience of love during an encounter as described earlier as the "I-Thou" encounter and relationship which is at the core of love. These experiences are episodic in nature. They happen from time to time. They do not happen every moment of every day. Even if we have a long-term loving relationship with another person, the actual direct experiences of that love occurs as a result of individual acts.

The other experience of love is when we remember our experiences of love and remember the person we love. Those events can be remembered and thought about at any time and do not require a direct and immediate encounter with the person we love. Remembrances of the reality of love inspire us to seek more encounters of love. Remembrances of love sustain us when we are not with the one or ones we love. But remembrances are just that, memories of an individual or individuals whom we love. It is not the actual reality of love.

Since the actuality of love comes in and through encounters with the other person or persons, such encounters must be regularly sought and engaged in. Otherwise, the love dies. Memory alone will not sustain love. The memory of love experienced in the past will only sustain people for some finite period. The trouble with many people when it comes to love is that they do encounter each other and connect at the depth of each other as persons. In the case of a woman and a man, that encounter often leads to a desire to be with that person in a special way and for a long time. Typically, those two people get married. The difficulty comes when time moves on and the two people no longer have the person to person encounters of love that they initially experienced. They expect the memories of their love to sustain them forever. Unfortunately, it does not work that way. And then people fall out of love.

Love exists.

I know it through experience.

I believe in it as well in the sense that I believe I will continue to love and be loved in the future. I don't know that for sure. But I believe I will continue to experience the reality of love as my life moves forward. Hopefully, I will sustain the love I now experience with those with whom I now have a loving relationship (my wife, my children, my brothers and sisters, my friends). I hope too, that as I meet more individuals in the future, I will be able to build and sustain loving relationships with them.

I know love. I believe in love. And, consequently, I make decisions and choices in my life based on this knowledge of and belief in love.

Love is also tied to knowledge and belief in my experience because of my encounters with people I have had a loving relationship with over the years. Part of the "I-Thou" encounter that Buber talks about is the uniquely human experience of connecting with the total oneness of body and spirit that constitutes ourselves and every other human being who exists.

Finally, that encounter and connection with another human being is something that I think also applies to our belief-based relationship with God. There is a wonderful line in one of the songs in the musical, "Les Miserables" that I think captures what I am trying to say about love, knowledge, and belief. The line is "to love another person is to see the face of God." When we love and encounter another person as I have described it, we encounter and experience a body and spirit togetherness and oneness that is similar to, and a foreshadowing of, our encounter and connection to God.

CHAPTER FIVE

The Most Basic Question: Why is There Something Instead of Nothing?

Why is there something instead of nothing?

The answer to that question sets the framework for answering many other questions that human beings have wrestled with forever, such as:

Is there a God?

If so, what or who is God?

What am I?

Who am I?

Why am I here?

How do I relate to, and fit into, the rest of reality?

How should I live my life to be happy?

The list of questions can go on and on; and, as this book continues, the list of questions will grow. I hope, too, that some answers, or at least some inkling of answers, will emerge also.

So, getting back to the first question, "Why is there something instead of nothing?"

Many people answer by saying "So what," or "Who cares?" The total reality in which we find ourselves is simply there. It just is.

"Why does the universe exist?" and "How did it get here?" are questions which most people do not think about on a regular basis. Or if they do think about them at all, they say that it is unimportant to know; or they say that the answer to the question is unknowable, so why waste time thinking about it.

In my judgment, it is not a waste of time to think about the question of "Why is there something instead of nothing?" The answer to that question forms the basis of our judgments about many other aspects of our lives including, but not limited to: how we live; the moral or ethical choices we make; our relationships with other people; and finally, the ultimate meaning of each of our own lives.

My answer to the question of "Why is there something instead of nothing?" is that some thing, some being, some power, some *something* more than likely created the reality within which we live.

"Nothing comes from nothing" is an old axiom that seems to be self-evident.

No matter what we see around us in the material universe we experience every day, all of the things, both great and small, exist only because they were caused by and/or were preceded by some other elements of material reality. For example:

- Our current universe was created by the event we call the "Big Bang."
- The creation of a new human being begins with the union of an egg and a sperm.
- Chocolate brownies are made from a recipe containing many ingredients.
- Electricity comes about through a number of physical processes and elements interacting together.

The list of examples is endless. There is simply not one thing that exists in the material universe that does not have its causation in some other material reality.

Science has made great strides in assisting all of us to understand the constituent parts and causation processes of material reality. For example, atoms contain protons, electrons, and neutrons; these in turn contain baryons and mesons which contain quarks and leptons; these in turn are affected by the strong force, weak force, gravitational force, gluons and bosons. Eventually, even more minute and fundamental particles, forces, and processes will probably be discovered.

But no matter how small scale our analysis becomes, as in the case of the constituent components and processes of an atom, or how large scale our analysis becomes, as in the case of the entire universe from the "Big Bang" to the expanding universe we observe today, all aspects of the material reality we experience everyday arc caused by some other, preceding material reality.

So, go back and ask yourself the question again. If nothing comes from nothing in the material world we experience every day, why is there something instead of nothing? What caused the material universe to come into existence in the first place?

I think there can only be two answers.

One answer is that there is no need for an answer to that question. There is no need for some type of cause or creator. There is an infinite regression in material causes. The universe as we know it just is!

I think that answer just evades the question. It is intellectually and experientially unsatisfying to me.

The second answer is that there is some type of non-material entity or being which created something from nothing.

Both answers are unprovable.

But my experience of reality tells me that the second answer makes more sense than the first answer. There is nothing that I know of in this material universe that does not have some type of material cause. Therefore, the only way that any material universe could have come into being is if a non-material or spiritual entity or being created it.

Human beings generally refer to that ultimate, non-material entity or being as God, the first cause, the creator, etc.

Whether creation took place at the only "Big Bang" we are currently aware of or at one or more previous contractions and expansions of the material universe, at some point the material universe came into being.

How that happened is the basic question of our understanding of reality.

To paraphrase Blasé Pascal, a betting man after my own heart, he once said that there is either a god or not a god. He was betting that there is a god. And he also decided that he really had nothing to lose on the bet if there is not a god.

Again, I can't prove that there is a god. But the fact that I choose to say there is a god does not mean that I am irrational and living in a world of make-believe.

From a logical and experiential basis, it is a more plausible judgment, a more credible judgment, that a non-material being created the material universe than the judgment that the material universe simply exists with no cause or explanation of how it came into being.

My knowledge and experience of reality is that it is more credible to say that there is a spiritual being that created material reality than to say that material reality has just always existed and needs no explanation. I think and believe I am right. I have bet my life on it, because what I think and believe plays a big part in how I lead my life.

So my answer to the question, "Why is there something instead of nothing?" is that there is a spiritual entity or being that created a material universe.

And that leads to the next question: "What is this spiritual entity or being like?"

CHAPTER SIX

Limits to and History of Talking About God

If there is some type of spiritual entity or being which is the cause of material reality coming into existence, then how can we describe this spiritual entity?

Many human beings, in their quest to understand the universe they live in, have called that entity God.

The first thing we need to remember when we talk about God is that our language is limited because so much of our knowledge and experience is based on our everyday interactions with reality as we see it as human beings. Whatever we say about God has to be understood as coming from our perspective as human beings. As discussed previously, our knowledge of things in our own plane of existence is usually incomplete. Our talk about God has to be understood as only expressing partial knowledge about an entity whose total reality is beyond our direct knowledge and experience.

Humans have struggled to describe god or gods for as far back as any type of historic record exists. In western civilization, the descriptions begin with ancient Egyptian dynasties of 2000 B.C. or earlier, through Homer's Greek gods, through the God of the Old and New Testaments, through the Koran and Allah, up to and including the "New Age" descriptions of the last 25 years. In eastern civilization, Buddhism, Confucianism, Shintoism and many other religions have also tried to describe god and/or gods.

I think that all of the past and current religious traditions and theologies tell us something about God. I don't think any of them capture the total and complete nature of what God is. I certainly am not presumptuous enough to think that I am going to capture and describe the totality of God. I read somewhere that the last words of St. Thomas Aquinas, recognized as one of the great and learned Catholic theologians who wrote extensively about God, were to the effect that "all I have written to date is like straw." What that meant was that he realized the more and more he thought about and experienced God in his own life, his words were inadequate to express the reality that is God.

As we move forward in the rest of this chapter, I am going to talk about God primarily from the western civilization and Judeo-Christian perspective. It is what I know best. By doing so, I am admitting and clearly exemplifying my statement above that God is too big and too different of a reality for us humans to fully capture. What I will say below in no way negates or contradicts the descriptions and images of God as developed by other cultures. But from a practical standpoint, I need to have some working concept of God in order for me to live my life and make decisions with the best chance of making good decisions within the framework of knowledge, belief, and love discussed previously.

When talking about God, some frequent language and images of God are as follows: God the Father…God Almighty…God All-Knowing…God the Creator…God is the Judge…the wrath of God… "Sinners in the hands of an angry God"…God sends his Son to suffer and die for us so that He (God) is appeased and we are saved…God condemns sinners to hell! Certainly these are awe inspiring descriptions, but also pretty scary. They are also pretty negative. What kind of God sends His Son to die for sinners so that He (God) is appeased? Is this a God we want to be close to? Is this someone we want to spend eternity with? I guess it beats going to hell, but it would probably be best to stay out of His sight if and when we do make it to heaven. It is sort of like living with a mean drunk. They can explode at any time based on their moods.

Another set of language and images are: God is love…The Lord is my Shepherd…Jesus is God and Jesus went about healing the sick, giving sight to the blind, raising the dead to life. Jesus preached a new commandment, "Love your neighbor as you love yourself." God is Wisdom…the Holy Spirit who will fill you with peace and joy. These images and descriptions are positive and life-affirming. They are not as frequently presented as the first set of images, but they do show other aspects of our perceptions of God.

Part of the problem when talking about God derives from the historical realities of when and where Christianity developed. The Christian tradition was developed within a Jewish patriarchal and hierarchical society that functioned within a Roman Empire operating under Roman law which had Greek philosophy as its underlying intellectual base. Consequently, many of the images of God in Christianity are of a male, kingly, judgmental God. Those images served Christianity well as it struggled to gain a foothold in a patriarchal, hierarchical, juridical/legalistic culture. They also served in establishing the power structure of the Christian church during the first centuries of its existence.

The language of patriarchy, hierarchy, and judgment, though giving us a view of some aspects of God, are inadequate and in many ways misleading and harmful. God the Father language and imagery have pretty much institutionalized male domination of religion and culture. That does not mean that male imagery and language caused the domination at its inception. At the time Christianity started, male domination in Roman, Greek, Hebrew, and most other western and Middle Eastern societies was the prevailing culture. But it does mean that such language and imagery have contributed to the long-term marginalization of women in Christian churches as well as in secular political, economic, and cultural aspects of society. Basically, male dominated language and imagery have robbed individuals and society of the values, talents, and skills of half of the population prior to and through the Christian era. Also, for many people, fathers have not been a very positive experience and relationship. Many fathers have been bad fathers over the years. They did not communicate with, or care about, their children. They treated their mothers badly. They were harsh and arbitrary.

God as King is again reflective of the times when Christianity came into being. "Kingness" contains an interesting set of images and accompanying language. Most of them are not positive for those who are not kings (pretty much 99.999999% of human beings). Most kings in history left a lot to be desired. If you were one of the lucky ones to have a good king, then language and images of a just king, a protective king, a powerful and awesome king, a saving king, a king that shared his bounty with his subjects resonated positively with that small minority of subjects. Kings, of course, were also male. That fit together nicely with the father image for those who were male and kings. And if you were male, but not a king, it was at least better to be at least like the king in your maleness.

God as Judge...The terrible swift sword...Sinners in the hands of an angry God...the imagery and language associated with God as a judge of the living and the dead has been generally fear-inducing and has been used to control individuals and groups. I am not saying that human beings do not do evil things to each other. I also am not saying that human beings do not need some standards of right and wrong, and be held accountable for their behavior. And I do think that some time there will be a day of reckoning for each of us where we will need to painfully grow into the full humanity for which we are created (I will talk about this topic at greater length in a subsequent essay). But judgment/condemnation language is not inspiring language. It is a language of fear. It is a language of guilt, which is necessary to a certain degree, but which has been used by people in power to retain their power and is often experienced by individuals to a debilitating effect.

Though the above images and language regarding God are accepted by many, I find them too confining and, frankly, pretty negative. I am sure they are comforting to some people. But I think overall, that they do a disservice to God and to people. The biggest disservice, in my judgment, is that they create a world view that is based on male oriented, non-interpersonal, power relationships. They create an absolutist mind set and way of thinking. They result in many people rejecting God because the language of power and control cannot answer questions about evil and bad things happening in the world. "How could God allow the Holocaust?" "How could God allow small children to die of cancer?"

I don't presume to have complete answers to these and many other questions. But I think that there are other images and language about God that are more appropriate and are better able to answer some of these questions than the traditional power, control, and judgmental images of God.

CHAPTER SEVEN

What I Think About God

First of all, I think about God as the Creator...the Being that brought into existence the material reality in which we exist.

Second, I see God as a knowing Being...a Being that has knowledge and understanding.

Third, I see God as a choosing/deciding Being.

Four, I see God as a loving Being...a Being that is

-Relational

-Mutually open to and accepting of human beings

-Desires and acts for the well-being of human beings

-Desires to be one with human beings

God is a Creative...Knowing...Choosing...and Loving Being.

From skeptics, the response to the above is probably: "Well, isn't that convenient? Doesn't that make life more bearable in a self-delusionary way of thinking? Aren't you just projecting your own life experiences, language, and hopes onto some fairytale being?"

Frankly, I am a pretty skeptical person myself. That is why I have spent so much time reading and thinking about God. And, yes, some of my ideas are projections of my hopes and desires. Then again, the fact that we hope for and desire certain things (like love, as an example) does not mean that they are not real.

I see God as The Creator because of the reasons I set forth in an earlier chapter.

I see God as knowing because a creator needs to have some type of knowledge and intelligence. It doesn't have to be the same way of knowing and the same types of knowledge that we are used to in human terms. But it seems reasonable that, if a God exists, God would possess knowledge.

I see God as choosing and deciding, because that is what a creative and knowing being does. It (God) chooses to do or not do (sounds a little like Yoda). Again, this is a projection of our human language and images. It doesn't have to be the same way of choosing and deciding that we experience as human beings. But I think it is reasonable that if God exists, is a creator, and contains/possesses knowledge, then God is capable of choosing.

Being creative, intelligent, and capable of choosing are attributes that we can reasonably attribute to God. I think it is reasonable to say that if the creatures of the Creator are capable of knowing and choosing, then so is the Creator.

Finally, to me, God is a Loving Being. This is where faith, and particularly the Christian faith, has a significant impact on my ideas about God.

Saying that God is a Loving Being is more of a faith-based assertion than the other three attributes. I don't think it is an unreasonable thing to say and believe. I think as human beings we have the capability and capacity to love. I think it is reasonable to say that the Creator of a universe that has resulted, among many other things, in human beings that are capable of love, is also capable of love.

Though I have said several times above the attributes of creating, knowing, choosing, and loving are reasonable to ascribe to God because God's creatures exhibit such characteristics, I don't ascribe all of our human characteristics to be a part of Who God is, particularly the negative and destructive characteristics of human beings. I expect God to be good and to be perfect. I expect God to be the ultimate good.

I do not expect God to be or do evil. That does not preclude ascribing to God some type of "anger" with the evil that we do. I do have a problem with that anger being described as wrathful and vindictive. Anger that leads to recognizing evil and then taking positive action to change the evil actions or results of others wrongdoing is a good thing.

Very importantly, I see God as a relational Being rather than a top down, directive Being relative to human beings.

Just as we are significantly formed and developed as human beings by our relationships to others, so too are we affected by our relationship with God.

In many ways, I am who I am because of the relationships with other human beings during my lifetime. I am also who I am based on my gene pool and my other life experiences. I will change and become different in many ways in the years ahead due to both my relationships and experiences. As I get older, I will also be changed as my physical being changes (and as the last 10 years of my life has taught me, probably not for the better from a physical standpoint).

I am who I am, as well, because of my relationship with God. I believe that I do have a person to person relationship with God that is somewhat like the person to person relationship I have with the human beings I know and love. It is like having a trusted and good friend. Someone you can rely on to look out for and act for your well-being. Someone with whom you have an I-Thou relationship. It is like having a relationship with a person who gives you advice, perspective, a true reading to yourself of who you are, honestly, and from the perspective that they love you and want the best for you.

When we give ourselves to another and that person gives themselves to us, it is just that...a gift. It is one of the most wonderful gifts we can give and receive. I believe that we can all have that same encounter and loving relationship with God. We have to be open to it. We have to pursue it. We have to seek it out. We must develop and nourish that relationship just like we do with other human beings. It is a two-way street.

God is more than I can conceive. But that does not mean God is more than I can relate to and experience.

Just as my human relationships of love are real, but not totally definable; so, too, is my relationship with God.

And my God is a God who is creative, intelligent, choosing, and loving…a Person.

It may be wishful thinking. But I think and believe it is real, as best as I can understand it within my basic premise, that there is a God instead of there not being a God, just as there is something instead of nothing.

CHAPTER EIGHT

Change, Evolution, and God

Change occurs every second of every day.

Changes happen within us, are brought about by us, or occur outside of us with or without our intention or cooperation.

One of the real advancements in science over the last century is the discovery of constant change. Whether it is chaos theory, the expanding universe, the theory of relativity, or the theory of evolution, everything points to constant change both in reality and how we perceive that reality.

Some people think that change and evolution is random, contingent, and just plain, dumb luck. Flowing out of this set of ideas is the world-view that there really is no meaning to anything beyond what we can sensibly experience in a material world. There is no ultimate purpose. Reality is just a crapshoot. Things that flourish are those that are best adapted to the environment in which they exist. For some, it is a world where the survival of the fittest is the ruling principle. Finally, within this world-view, humans are not any higher or lower in the hierarchy of beings than any other being. We are just one of many entities which evolved over time and probably, like the dinosaurs, will eventually become extinct.

Others think there is an intelligent design and designer that has not only created a universe governed by laws, but also intervenes at times in the material universe to create new entities, particularly human beings. Within this world-view, there are people who totally reject change as set forth in evolutionary theory as it applies to humans. They also reject change and evolution as expressed in the "Big Bang" theory or even the fossil record where they contend that God created the universe about 6,000 or so years ago and created fossils and layers of sediment in rocks, and other examples of reality which point to a universe which is somewhere between fifteen and twenty billion years old. In any case, and no matter where groups or individuals fall on the spectrum of Intelligent Design/Creationism, this world-view considers human beings to be direct creations of God. Human beings are seen as the pinnacle of creation. Human beings are seen as special. They see evolution and related social theories, such as survival of the fittest, as dangerous to society and an affront to God.

Ideas have consequences. That is why there is such a battle between science and religion over questions and theories related to change and evolution. On one side there are scientific materialists who think and believe that there is no reality beyond the material reality they can measure and verify. On the other side, there are mainly religious people who see scientific materialism as a threat to important values that emphasize the dignity and worth of every person, the goodness of sharing and caring for those who are not the "fittest," and the purposefulness of life.

As usual, I see elements of truth in both sides of the argument. Also, as usual, I do not think there are only two viewpoints on the subject.

I have to say that I share the fear of many intelligent design advocates that an arbitrary, survival of the fittest philosophy that has been popularly connected to Darwin's theory of evolution is scary. There have been too many examples in the 20th century that have embodied and carried out that philosophy in the worst possible ways: eugenic experiments and controls; the many horrors of Nazism and

Fascism; way too many genocides; and, the on-going, no-holds-barred capitalism that redistributes the majority of wealth and resources to the richest few while putting the environment at risk for future generations.

On the other hand, I have no problem with evolution as a theory. I have read many books on the subject. And though I am not a trained scientist, it seems to have a strong basis in proven and tested experiments and facts. Granted, there are gaps in the fossil record and that nothing has been directly observed regarding the types of significant, natural selection Darwinism purports. But at this point in time, it seems like a pretty solid theory as the result of "the convergence, neither sought nor fabricated, of the results of work that was conducted independently," as stated by Pope John Paul II a few years ago.

My own opinion is that there is a God as I have set forth previously. This God created the material world in which we exist. There are "laws" or regular patterns in the universe that affect many natural processes (physical, chemical, and biological). Whether these "laws" were actually set up or not by God is an open question in my mind. However, through billions of years of interactions, certain elements and processes of the cosmos began to survive better than others. Eventually, a certain order was established. But at the same time as there is a general order within the universe, there are also instances and circumstances that release or unleash chaos in the universe today. Science has found that all scientific laws are not immutable. There are variabilities and irregularities in how things happen.

So I do not see God as necessarily the Intelligent Designer or the Big Clockmaker in the sky. Could be, but I don't know for sure. I think it is just as rational and intelligible to think that God created some basic material realities (maybe at the Big Bang 15 billion years ago or maybe at a previous Big Bang 15 billion years before that) and lets the universe evolve and change as elements and processes interact. Such a view even allows for parallel universes or universes that preceded ours and will succeed ours. It is possible that as these elements and processes interacted that intelligent life evolved in our universe and maybe it has done so, or will do so, in other universes.

I think the crux of the problem between scientific materialists and intelligent designers is not how the material world developed/changed/evolved. The real problem is that the scientific materialists see no evidence of a god or of any spiritual realities which exist and are part of the bigger picture. That is okay in my book, because scientists are only observing, measuring, and describing the material world. They can properly say that the scientific method and knowledge does not allow for any knowledge which is not learned through their particular disciplines. And since spirit, however defined, is not of a material nature, then they cannot speak to its existence from their frame of reference. All of that is fine with me. However, I think they go too far when they say that their method of learning and knowing is the only way of knowing and learning that we as human beings are able to utilize as discussed earlier in Chapter 2. They go too far in saying there is no God because they cannot prove God's existence by their mode of research and thinking.

The intelligent designers/creationists are mistaken in either denying the abundance of scientific evidence about change and evolution or in saying that their science proves the existence of God. Nothing proves the existence of God from a scientific, reductionist approach to knowledge. The laws of science, and the beauty and complexity of different aspects of the universe from the large to the small, may point to the possibility of an Intelligent Designer, but they don't prove it.

Taking into account what I said in the previous chapter, I see change, evolution, and God as fitting together quite well.

I think that part of the problem of reconciling the dichotomy between change, evolution, and a loving God is that many of the biblical images of God are too narrow and anthropomorphic. All images of God are human constructions that limit the reality of God to something we are familiar with. The traditional images of God as omnipotent, patriarchal, monarchical, and rational, are too limiting to address the issues raised in the last one hundred and fifty years not only by evolution, but also by the theory of relativity, chaos theory, and quantum physics as well. God as a kingly male, a control freak, may appeal to some, but it does not answer questions raised by the last 150 years of scientific discoveries.

Different images of God and related theologies are necessary for us to successfully and positively deal with scientific discoveries and realties. I have previously suggested an image of a God of compassionate love that is with us, but separate from us…a God that is calling all of creation to a vision and a future that we all participate in creating. We are all co-creators of the future of the universe as change and evolution take place. We can stand on the sidelines and just let things happen or we can become engaged with reality and help shape and lead it to a better world.

A relational God of compassionate love beats the images of the theologians who see God as an all-powerful designer who wants order, and has control and power over the world and others. Those images are safe and make some people feel comfortable, while the opposite idea of living in an evolving and indefinite world for which we bear some responsibility can be scary and anxiety producing.

The imagery of love, compassion, and co-creation also beats the fatalistic and pessimistic image of the evolutionary materialists who think humans are an interesting, random result of chemical and biological processes, and nothing else. They are probably right that human beings are the result of those evolutionary processes. But scientifically speaking, that is all they can and should say about human beings. Why we are here and who we really are as human beings is beyond the purview of scientific inquiry.

How and what we think about God has a large role to play in how and what we think about human beings and the morality and ethics of interacting with each other. If God does not exist, then we are only a complex sack of chemicals and biological processes. There is really no reason to act as if a human being is something worth respecting and treating with dignity and love. Along the same lines, if we are just playing out a game set up by the big Designer in the sky, we really are not responsible for helping to create a better, more loving world. Rather, it is better to be safe and make sure we follow the Boss's orders so we are not left out of the world to come.

But if God is a relational, compassionate, and loving Being that has made us free to be part of the on-going process of creation, then we should be faithfully and actively engaged in the creative process - a process that is risky, but if approached with love and humility, will make us more god-like and the world a more beautiful and exciting creation.

CHAPTER NINE

What and Who Am I?

I am a being, an individual entity. I exist. I am certain of that as I am that I am sitting in this chair and typing this sentence.

For sure, I am a material being. I am a physical body (I almost wanted to say I *have* a physical body. But to say I *have* a body would say that the material elements of who I am are of lesser importance than the spiritual element of who I am).

As a physical body, I am a complex conglomeration of many integrated chemical, biological, and physical elements and systems (I use the term physical not only in the sense of a corporeal being, but also in the sense of the physical interactions of entities such as those present in elements of electricity and motion, and other aspects of physics).

In some ways, I am an electronic being. My heartbeat is governed by electric impulses. My brain makes connections through a multitude of electronic charges and synapses, and sends electrical impulses throughout my body to perform every bodily function necessary.

I have five senses by which I interact with the world around me. The interactions are chemical, biological, and physical.

I am a learning and knowing being. I have a brain which has tremendous capabilities of processing a continuous flow of information that results from my body interacting with all kinds of other physical realities.

I am a self-aware being. I know not only how I feel and what I am thinking at any particular time, but I also know that I know those things. I can sort of sit back and look at myself from the outside, almost like a third person character in a story. Right now I am typing this sentence. I know and am aware that I am typing this sentence. I know that I feel good about typing this sentence and the other sentences in this book because I enjoy getting my thoughts down on paper, and because I hope that someday, someone else will read these words and find them helpful.

I have an imagination. I can think of possibilities that no one else may ever have thought about. I can think of and create realities that never existed before.

I am an evaluating being. I can look at the pros and cons of situations and understand what is good for me or not good for me.

I am a social being, an interactive being. I would not exist without the physical interaction of my parents. I could not continue to exist without interacting with other human beings on a regular basis. I need to interact with all of reality in order to exist and flourish.

I am a being in time. I change all of the time. I undergo physical change whether it is something as small as skin cells falling off and being replaced by new cells, or something more noticeable like all of the changes associated with the aging process. I change as I learn new things. Certainly the synapses and neurons in my brain change as I learn new things. But also, how I act and interact with reality changes because of what I learn. I change emotionally because of my life experiences. Change is constant in me and around me.

At the same time that all of this change is taking place, there is an essential "me-ness" that changes in some ways, but always has a

strong element of sameness. I have the sense or knowledge or awareness of myself that I am still "me," no matter what changes I am
impacted by from the outside or how I change my behavior through
time. That sense and awareness of who I am at my core is what I have
interpreted as the "I" that I referred to earlier as described by Martin
Buber. That sense and awareness of who another person is at their
core is the "Thou" as described by Buber.

The biggest change of all, of course, is that some day, I will die.
Unlike any other being I know of, I know I will die.

That is what I know at the far right side of the knowledge continuum. Scientific investigation can confirm all of the above state-
ments about me as a human being.

From a non-scientific, non-reductionist mode of thinking, I
think and believe I am a spiritual being. Not a spirit or soul *in* a body,
not a spirit that *has* a body, but a unique combination of material and
spiritual reality which we call a human being. I think and believe that
the body and spirit unite as one as the body develops a complex sub-
strate that is capable of uniting with the spirit.

I don't know how the body and spirit unite as one and when that
occurs. Though the Catholic Church now teaches that such a union
takes place at the moment of conception by an individual act of creation by God, I do not think, nor has the Catholic Church always
taught, that such is the case, at least in regards to the timing. I tend
to think of the union occurring as more of an evolutionary process.
As the body becomes more developed, particularly the brain and central nervous system, the body unites with the spirit. It may occur as
a particular, creative act of God. Or, it may occur as the body and
brain become complex enough to unite with, and participate in, the
spiritual reality which is part of the total cosmic reality that I
described in the first chapter of this book.

I am not bothered that I do not know when and how this unity occurs and becomes real. As I have said several times before in this book, there is much more to reality than we see, know, and experience. Our lack of knowledge and our lack of being able to physically apprehend and be in touch with all of reality that is out there is probably one of the most important things I have learned over the years. Reality is too complex and non-sensory to our limited physical beings to assume that all reality is of a material nature. That all of reality is encompassed in the material is a possibility, but it is only one possibility. It is also possible that spiritual, and even other realities that are not subject to our sense-based way of knowing, exist in us and around us. I think it will be wonderfully exciting in the future to learn about and know these realities which are not limited by our sense-based way of knowing material realities. Two hundred years ago, we knew nothing of the speed of light, the makeup of the atom, the theory of relativity, and so many more things that human beings have discovered which at the time, were simply beyond the comprehension of any human being. I hope I am still alive when another layer of reality is discovered and can be studied and learned about.

I am a choosing being. I can make choices that are not simply based on what is for my personal benefit. I can move beyond self-interest as the sole calculus of my decisions and choices. I can choose what is good for another because it is good for the other person. Though my history and genes may point me in a certain direction as far as making choices is concerned, I can freely choose to do things that are for a greater good beyond my own self-interest. That doesn't mean that I always consciously do that. But I do have that capability and I do make such choices.

I can also choose to do bad or evil things. I know that many people think that the terms bad or evil are relative terms. What might be bad in your eyes might be good in mine, and vice-versa. But I really think that there are some objective bad or evil things that all of us are capable of choosing and doing. I will talk more about evil later in these essays. At this point, I just want to say that all of us are capable of doing bad or evil things. We are not perfect beings or beings on the way to being perfect. We are not perfectible, but we are improvable. And to be a better person is a choice we can make. Just as we can make the choice to do harm.

I am a being capable of loving another person and being loved. It is a love that includes the physical interactions and manifestations of love, but also includes the ability to encounter the unique other or Thou that exists in another person. I can form a special connection and bond with another person. And, at the opposite end of the spectrum, I can hate. I can choose to do evil, to do harm to another person (physically or psychologically hurt them) or another being (torture an animal), or another physical entity (pollute the environment).

I am a human person. I have a unique blend of genes, history, spirit and body that has value in and of itself. There never has been, nor will be, an individual human being exactly like me, or like you, or like anyone else who ever existed. All human beings share much in common, but we all have a uniqueness about us. We have a separateness about us that we alone are knowledgeable of and aware of. No matter how hard we try, we can never totally communicate that uniqueness, that subjective knowledge of ourselves, to others.

I think we want to share our personhood with others. That is why we all want to experience love in the fullest human sense as I described it earlier and restate it below.

I respect, appreciate and enjoy my personhood. I try to do the same with the other persons I interact with on a daily basis.

From a strictly faith-based perspective, I am made in the image and likeness of God. To me, that means I am capable of knowing, choosing, and loving, because that is how I have described God in an earlier chapter.

What distinguishes a human being, a human person, from every other creature and entity we know about so far are these three elements:

- We know and we know that we know.
- We can freely choose between different courses of action.
- We can love and be loved in a mutually intentional, person-to-person encounter.

Only a human being has self-aware knowledge. I think other beings such as animals have brains and are capable of knowing and learning things. But I have seen no evidence that they have the capability of self-reflective knowledge that a human being has.

Only a human being can freely choose between different courses of action. I think animals do not choose their actions. I don't think that they can choose, because they do not have the self-reflective thought processes that we experience as human beings. Animals respond to a stimulus and engage in a course of action which is learned as a response to certain stimuli. As human beings, we also, sometimes or often, respond to stimuli with learned behavior. But that is not always the case. We can choose to respond differently than what our genes, or history, or past experiences point us towards.

Only human beings can love as I have described it previously and below. Though people often talk about loving their pets and their pets loving them, I do not think that animals have the capability of experiencing and choosing to encounter another being as love is described below:

- **A relational connection** between two people that is
- **Mutually open to and accepting** of the other person,
- **Desires and acts for the well-being of the other** person, and has at its core,
- The **desire to be one** with that person.

A human being's relationship with a pet can be an affectionate relationship. It can provide emotional satisfaction to both parties in the relationship. Each can be of value to the other as a result of the relationship, but there is not a conscious, self-reflective, self-aware choice by the pet to be in the relationship. It is a relationship between two different levels of being that hinges primarily on the conscious choice of the human being.

So, in answer to the question of "What and who am I?" I respond as follows:

I am a human person in time who is a unique combination of body and spirit, with a particular history, who exists in relationship to other things and people, and who has the capacity of:

- Learning and knowing.
- Self-awareness, subjective knowledge, self-consciousness… knowing that I know.
- Imagination and creativity.
- Evaluating and choosing.
- Loving and being loved.
- Dying and knowing I will die.

CHAPTER TEN

Why Am I Here?

I am here to fully participate in the realities in which I exist.

There are two important and distinct elements in that sentence.

The first element is to "fully participate." Those words denote action and activity on my part within the context of all of the elements of what and who I am as discussed in the previous chapter.

The second element is "the realities in which I exist." Those words denote the total environment in which I act, some basics of which have been described in the first seven chapters.

To fully participate means that I use all of the powers and capacities that I have as a human person in time who is a unique combination of body and spirit, with a particular history, who exists in relationship to other things and people, and who has the capacity of:

- Learning and knowing.
- Self-awareness, subjective knowledge, self-consciousness…knowing that I know.
- Imagination and creativity.
- Evaluating and choosing.
- Loving and being loved.
- Dying and knowing I will die.

The more actions I take that are in accord with what and who I am, the more I will flourish as a human being. I will grow and develop as an individual. I will help others grow and develop as human beings as well.

I don't use an apple to pound in a nail. The chances of success are non-existent. I pretty much will destroy the apple and no progress will be made in getting the nail to penetrate two boards and hold them together. It is not in the nature of an apple to serve as a hammer.

I think it is somewhat similar when I think and make decisions about how I should live as a human being. The more I take actions and live in accord with what and who I am as a human being, the better chance I have to live a flourishing life.

But I do not live in a vacuum. I live in a world of distinct otherness. So I not only need to know who and what I am and act accordingly. I also need to know and understand the realities with which I interact so that I can also act appropriately in response to the reality of the other.

In one sense, the other reality outside of myself demands a certain response which is proper to who or what that other is. Just as I expect to be treated in a certain way (with respect, with dignity, with an appreciation of my uniqueness and singular personhood) and will flourish if so treated, the other with whom I am interacting demands the same response from me. The better and more completely I know the reality outside of myself, the better I can respond to and interact with that reality so that both of us entities flourish and accomplish our purpose, whether we are interacting with an apple or another human being.

So my answer to the question, "Why am I here?" has three main elements:

- Flourish as a human being.
- Contribute to the well-being and flourishing of others.
- Co-create the future of the universe.

Pretty heady stuff! Very challenging! Very exciting! Not easy!

To flourish as a human being, I need to develop and maintain all of the aspects of my being to the best of my ability. I need to take care of my body. I need to learn things constantly. I need to be in loving relationships with other human beings. I need to act appropriately in response to the realities within me and the realities outside of myself.

To contribute to the well-being and flourishing of others, I need to encounter and engage individuals with an understanding of who each one is as an individual. I need to make conscious choices to choose and act for the well-being of others as individuals and groups. I need to refrain from actions which harm others, but I need to more than avoid doing harm to others. I need to help create broad, structural organizations and institutions (physical, economic, and political) which will support the flourishing of others and myself.

To co-create the future of the universe, I need to engage with the rest of reality to make it better…to make it more hospitable to the growth and development of all aspects of reality. I need to do that not just in relationships with human beings, but with the environment as a whole within which we live, which includes all species of animal and vegetable life as well as the minerals, metals, water, etc., which make our lives now, and the lives of future generations, possible.

Very importantly, I need to balance what I do in all three areas listed above. Too much emphasis in one area can cause me and others harm.

Wanting to flourish as a human being, to reach my full potential as a human being, is a very worthwhile pursuit, but it cannot be the sole reason for everything I do. So many of the self-help and self-actualization gurus of today (Oprah and Dr. Phil to name a couple) focus everything on what is good for the self. In their world, even doing something good for someone else comes back to what is good for the self. If I do something good for someone else, then I feel good about myself or I just feel good, or I think I am a good person. All of those things may occur as a result of any particular act or series of acts. And that is fine.

But it is not the same as doing something good for another simply because they need it or they require it, or the reality of the situation demands it. People and things outside of ourselves have a claim on us as part of the total reality we all inhabit. As I discussed earlier, I, as an individual human being, expect and deserve to be treated with respect, dignity, and as worthy of time, attention, and resources. If I am not treated with that respect and dignity, then I am injured. For instance, if I am lying at the side of the road because I was hit by a vehicle and was left to die, the next person who comes along is almost compelled to respond to me and my situation, not because they will feel good about it or because some religion says they ought to do it. The situation demands that they stop and help me out as best they can. They may eventually get recognition for it. They may feel a sense of satisfaction as a result of helping me. But mainly, they have acted in a way that is appropriate for a human being to act in the particular situation that confronted them.

Non-human beings also have a claim on us. Animals should be treated humanely. Most of us recognize that torturing an animal is an inappropriate human action. At the same time, most of us recognize that the needs and claims of an animal for humane treatment do not preclude it being killed for food by another predator or a human being.

Inanimate objects demand a certain response from us. Our natural human reaction to seeing raw sewage dumped into a beautiful river is to stop that dumping if we can. Seeing someone preparing to destroy the Mona Lisa will move us to do what we can to stop that action from taking place. A beautiful sunset demands our attention. We stop to look at it almost involuntarily. In all of these responses to the realities outside of ourselves, there may be some self-interest that is served by our actions. But that is not and should not be the primary reason why we act for the well-being of the other realities outside of ourselves. Very importantly, it is what and who we are as human beings in relationship to any outside realities that almost requires us to act in a certain way which goes beyond our long or short term personal interests. And in acting that way in response to the realities outside of ourselves, we act appropriately as a human being. (I used the words "almost requires us" two sentences earlier because I think we can choose not to respond in an appropriate human way if we choose not to do so).

On the other hand, we cannot always put others first and ourselves last. We cannot always defer our hopes, dreams and desires in order to fulfill other's needs. Women, especially, have been expected to live such a life in the past and in many instances still today. They are expected to defer to the needs of their husbands and children. Always deferring because that is what the culture expects or from some religious motivation is not appropriate for a human being. It causes harm to the individual and the harm often spreads to those around them.

So balancing decisions and actions between what is good for me and what is good for others is important. There is no exact road map regarding how, when and to what degree it is appropriate to choose my well-being over someone else's. Often, there is no conflict. What is good for me in a situation can be good for the other as well. But other times there may be conflicts between what is good for me and what is good for the other. Sometimes I will discuss and evaluate the situation with the other person and decide that in a particular instance, it is best to choose what is best for me. Other times, I may evaluate the situation with the other person and decide that it is best for the other person to receive the benefit of some action, even though I might suffer some deprivation in the process. Sometimes there is a compromise solution where we both benefit to some degree and both experience a certain amount of deprivation or non-fulfillment.

Finally, I think it is important that to flourish as a human being, I need to have an element in my life which is bigger than myself. That excites my imagination. That pulls me out of myself. That provides me a vision and hope for the future. I need to give and commit myself to something that is more than my own well-being. I have to give myself to something else in order to flourish as a human being. Again, not to the detriment or harm to myself, but as a way to be part of the larger world and to utilize and develop my human skills and abilities to a high degree.

Often, when we think and talk about committing ourselves to something outside of ourselves that is bigger than we are, we think of political, religious, or business success. Those are fine things and are legitimate goals to seek. And I have pursued all of these goals. In particular, I think committing to an active relationship with God is very important. If, as I have said earlier, I think and believe that God exists, and that God is in an active relationship with all of creation to bring it into being, to sustain it, and to bring it to perfection with our help, then it is appropriate for a human being to relate to God as best as any of us human beings can determine that to be.

Like any other relationship that we have with other beings, human and even animal, it takes time and effort to develop and maintain such a relationship with God. I will speak more specifically to the elements and activities involved in that relationship later in this book. Suffice it to say at this point, that just as the other realities which we encounter demand/require/deserve a certain appropriate human response from us, so does our relationship with God.

We can have a relationship with God because it makes us feel good, or feel safe or saved, or because we want something from God: health, success, good things for our children, world peace, etc. But more importantly, we should have a relationship with God because it is appropriate…it is right and fitting that we as human beings seek to know and love God. God is the ultimate reality. As a human being wishing to fully participate in and be in a relationship with all of reality, I am truly most human when I am in a relationship with God as well as all of the rest of reality I encounter daily.

Finally, when I think of human beings committing themselves to something bigger than themselves, I often think of Yitzhak Perelman in particular, or any great artist or virtuoso in general. I also think of Michael Jordan. Both Perelman and Jordan have lots of natural talent, but they became great because they gave part of their life over to their art or sport. They practiced, practiced, practiced! They committed themselves to achieving excellence. They had to sacrifice a lot to achieve that excellence. There were many things they were not able to pursue so that they could pursue excellence in their own performance, but also to pursue the excellence of their art or sport.

The things that I have committed myself to outside of myself are the following:

- My wife
- My children
- My work
- God

- Making the world a better place
- My extended family

I started this chapter on "Why Am I Here?" with the statement, "I am here to fully participate in the realities in which I exist."

Every person has to figure out their own purpose, the purpose that fits what and who they are, and responds to and engages with the realities with which they interact.

I think if each individual examines and thinks about themselves within the framework of the three elements listed below, they will have a better chance of living a good life, a happy life, and a meaningful life, which is to:

- Flourish as a human being.
- Contribute to the well-being and flourishing of others.
- Co-create the future of the universe.

CHAPTER ELEVEN

What is Happiness?

Thinking and reading about happiness has not been an academic exercise for me and I don't think is an academic exercise for others. I have thought a lot about happiness over the years because I was so unhappy with my life many years ago that I often contemplated suicide.

During that time, I started to seriously, almost desperately, think about what it means to be happy and then to do things that would make me happier. I think I have had some pretty good success. I consider myself to be one of the happier people I know. Of course, I am judging that by the external behaviors of other people, since I don't know most people at the depth that is necessary to really be able to make a reasonable judgment about whether or not they are happy.

Over the last 50 years, as I have continued to think about and pursue happiness, I have found that there are some important elements to attaining a happy life. They are the following:

1. We have to define happiness.
2. We have to know ourselves and the world of realities outside of ourselves.
3. We must actively pursue and work for those things that will make us happy.

We have to define happiness. What are we aiming at? How do we know we have achieved it? Is it different for different people?

Happiness is the long-term state or condition of human beings who are in harmony with all of the realities in us and around us.

It is more than a feeling of happiness, of feeling good all of the time. No one feels good all of the time. No one has only happy experiences in their lives. If we only consider ourselves to be happy when we feel elated, then we will seldom be happy. That is not to say that feeling happy is not part of being happy. It is just to say that the feelings of happiness are only part of the answer. Feelings are fleeting and changeable. They are not particularly controllable. Feelings are important in life and in achieving happiness. They just cannot be the sole object of what we are trying to attain in living a happy life.

Happiness is also more than experiencing pleasure. Our experience of pleasure is important to us as human beings. Pleasure draws us to activities which are important to our survival as individuals and as a species. But pleasure is not the same as happiness.

Happiness is a deeper reality than just how we feel at any particular time. It has a component of understanding our life and ourselves within a broader framework of reality over a period of time. Happiness is a state of being that is the result of a life well-lived...a life lived in harmony with the realities in us and around us. It has more of a sense of on-going contentment/satisfaction, peace, and joy to it more so than brief and fleeting moments of euphoria. Happiness is a life work. It results from looking at the big picture and the long run of one's life and making decisions and choices that have us engaging appropriately with reality.

Happiness has superficial as well as profound elements to it. By superficial, I mean the things in our life that are good to have, but without which we can still flourish as a human being. For instance, if I am on a team that wins the Super Bowl, that is a very joyous and happy event in my life. It is worth pursuing that goal. But if I never win the Super Bowl, I will not be less of a human being as I have defined it previously and I will not have a less happy life.

The superficial elements of happiness differ for many of us. I enjoy playing sports. I enjoy a good movie or a good book. I enjoy a good meal and a good wine. You may hate sports but enjoy dancing. You may enjoy conversations with others more than reading a book. I may like philosophy and you may enjoy entomology. Some people actually enjoy doing tax returns!

All of these different activities make us happy or unhappy because they are in harmony with who we are, and how we are most comfortable in interacting with the realities within us and outside of us. And they are very important components of our happiness. For example, I love music. It would make me happy to be able to play a musical instrument. I can't do it. I have tried many instruments many times over many years. I just have no musical talent whatsoever when it comes to playing an instrument. If I had to spend my entire life trying to be a good musician, I might attain a serviceable ability to do so. I might get good enough so people wouldn't run from the room as soon as I started to tickle the ivories. But I would not experience happiness in the short run or in the long run of my life if I equated being a good musician with being happy. On the other hand, I enjoy the music that other people can make. The way for me to be in harmony (no pun intended) with the realities of music is to listen to it and appreciate the talents of others who can produce beautiful music.

From a more profound standpoint, I think all of us are happy if we flourish as human beings as described in previous chapters. We are happy if we have sufficient amounts of the basics of life: food, clothing, shelter, a sense of safety. We are happy if our children flourish. We are happy if no one is shooting at us or our children, or blowing up bombs on the buses we ride. We have a more profound happiness if we are loved and love others. We are happy when we learn things, when we broaden our knowledge, when we understand things. I often remember the faces of students I have taught over the years as they struggled to understand something and then finally did understand it. It was like the proverbial light bulb going on. I could see the understanding occurring, and the subsequent joy and happiness in the eyes and faces of the students because they now knew something new.

Some things make us feel happy for a short time. Some things make us feel happy over the long run. The superficial things give us a feeling of happiness for the short term. The feelings of happiness related to acquiring and possessing things can be very strong, but usually those feelings last for a limited time. Also, acquiring and having things only satisfies us till we want more of something or the next new thing.

Profound things make us deeply happy over the long term. We have positive feelings of happiness when we think about and are engaged with the deeper, more profound, good things we have in our lives. And rather than being brief and fleeting feelings of happiness, they produce in us a deeper sense of peace, and joy, and satisfaction resulting from both an intellectual and emotional understanding of who we are and how we fit into the broader realities around us.

Having been loved by another person, even if that person has been dead for many years, can still give us a deep sense of happiness and satisfaction. On the other hand, the joy we experienced in getting a new car two years ago really no longer gives us much joy.

There is a difference in the happiness that is achieved through *having* things versus *becoming* more of a human being. Acquiring and having things (material goods, power, status, lovers, etc.) is important, up to a point.   Becoming more by growing as a human being (knowing more, loving and being loved more, having greater wisdom and compassion) is important in and of itself; and though there is always a desire to want more knowledge, love, and wisdom, it is not an unsettling, anxiety-producing, stressful set of desires that won't be eased until we attain more of any of these profound goods. Rather, it is a peaceful journey toward an optimistic goal of becoming more of what it means to be a human being.

What makes us unhappy is wanting, pursuing, and finally attaining what is not good for us…what is not in harmony with the realities inside and outside of ourselves.

We are told that what will make us happy is money, fame, sex, power, a big home, a fancy car, a plasma screen TV, and all of the other trappings of a successful life. All of us are bombarded these days with endless media messages about what is supposed to make us happier. Buy the right beer or car, or get the whitest teeth you can, and you will be happy! People of the opposite sex will want you.

Certainly, obtaining any and all of these things described above can produce a certain amount of enjoyment. And there is nothing wrong with wanting and acquiring some of these things and achieving some of these goals if they fit who we are and we do not harm others along the way. In truth, we need some of these things simply to survive. We all need a certain amount of material goods in order to have safe and healthy lives for ourselves.

But acquiring things provides only short term happiness and joy. And often, when we achieve a certain level of material goods or power or fame, we find out two things: first, the pleasure only lasts for a short time and afterward, we feel empty and unfulfilled; and two, we want and need more of these things to get the same rush of happiness we had when we previously achieved a particular goal.

So, if we spend our lives and energies acquiring things and pursuing goals that are not related to who and what we are as a human being, we ultimately will not be happy. We will be on an endless treadmill of acquiring and working to acquire things. And, of course, the more that we need, the more we have to work to acquire those things that will supposedly make us happy once we get to that next level of acquisition and consumption.

So, to restate, happiness is the long-term state or condition of human beings who are in harmony with all of the realities in us and around us.

CHAPTER TWELVE

What Does Knowledge Have to Do With Happiness?

In order to be happy, we have to know ourselves and the world of realities outside of ourselves. To do this we have to pursue two bodies of knowledge. One body of knowledge is about ourselves. It follows the dictum of the Greek philosopher who said, "Know thyself." The second body of knowledge is about the world of realities outside of ourselves. To do that requires us to be lifelong learners. Growing in both areas of knowledge are difficult and challenging tasks. Both take time. Both can be extremely rewarding. Both can be scary and disconcerting as well.

In regards to knowing ourselves, in the previous chapters I talked about what and who we are as a human being in general. I am not going to repeat those ideas here. To a lesser degree, I have also talked previously about who we are as individual, human persons.

Self-examination and evaluation of ourselves as individuals, taking into account our talents, temperament, and inclinations, is part of knowing ourselves as individuals. Not knowing ourselves as individuals opens the door to our being led by outside influences to define who we are and what will make us happy. Advertising, which has entered almost every phase of our lives, tries to do just that. It defines us as consumers and as people who will be happy if we have the "right" things which, in turn, will have us interact with people who will like us. Peer pressure from friends can also try to define who we are as individuals. Parents can try to define who a child is in many ways…how they expect them to behave…what goals they set for them…how they respect the individuality of the child…how much they project their own parental expectations and definitions of success onto their children. Religion, social groups, business, educational institutions, and many other forces try to tell us who we are, and, consequently, what we should have, do and be in order to be happy.

Suffice it to say, there are many individuals, groups, and cultural forces that try to define who we are as human beings in general and as a particular human being. All of these influences on our developing sense of ourselves are not necessarily bad or misleading. We do need to consume things. We need to have goals. We need to have friends. My point is that we cannot take the understanding and expectations of outside forces as the sole determinant of who we are as an individual. It takes thoughtful, self-reflection. It takes the study of a broad range of humanities and arts. It takes quiet time. And for me at least, it takes prayerful meditation as well.

The scary part for many of us in trying to understand ourselves is that it can be uncomfortable doing so. We may have an idea about ourselves, which as we learn more about ourselves, we may have to change. It takes self-discipline. We have to learn to be quiet. Not much in our society today encourages silence and thoughtful self-reflection and knowledge. So we have to separate ourselves from the crowd and the noise that constantly bombards our life. We have to learn new thinking skills. We have to get to know ourselves at the deepest level of who we are. Not just as someone who likes sports, or enjoys listening to music, or whatever other activity we pursue, but as someone who is a unique human person. None of this is easy. We are given very few examples and very little training in how to do this as we grow up. And, if we haven't learned it as we grow up, it becomes difficult in adulthood to even recognize that we do not really know ourselves. We continue to pursue things that we are told will make us happy, but may or may not do so unless they are in harmony with who we are as human beings in general and as a specific, individual, unique human being.

Finally, another fallacy that we are often told is that we can be anything we want to be…that there are no limitations on who and what we can be. It sounds good…very encouraging and empowering to people. But in reality, we can't be anything we want to be unless it fits who we are as an individual and very specific human being. We will not be a great musician if we don't have the talent. We won't be a great gymnast if we throw up every time we do a somersault. We won't be an NBA star if we are slow-footed and are 5 feet 2 inches tall. We all won't make a million dollars a year. Happiness depends on each of us knowing our talents and abilities in certain areas. Happiness also depends on a lot of outside variables and luck, both good and bad. That does not mean that we should not pursue such things. We just need to recognize somewhere along the line that we may not have the talents and skills to excel at certain things and then redirect our efforts to other goals that do fit us.

Knowing as much as we can about the realities outside of ourselves requires that we be lifelong learners. It is an absolute necessity to getting as true an understanding of reality as possible. Lifelong learning means not only practical and job-related learning, which is extremely important in the fast changing scientific, technical and economic world of today, it also means learning in terms of literature, history, art, music, philosophy and all of the other areas of learning that are classified under the broad category of the humanities. Lifelong learning is not to be limited to learning in an academic setting. The world is full of information, experiences, and personal interactions that we can encounter and learn from in almost limitless ways.

Like self-knowledge, lifelong learning can be scary. It means that we will have to change some of our ideas about a broad range of topics. It means that we might have made decisions and choices years ago which have shaped our life till now. And they may have been wrong decisions based on what we understand of reality today. That is very threatening to many people.

So, in order to truly be a lifelong learner, we have to be open to new ideas, not just from a theoretical standpoint or even a practical everyday life circumstances standpoint, but also from a deep, experiential, life-shaping standpoint. It is not easy. But I think we have a better chance of being happy.

In summary, we need to know ourselves and the realities outside of ourselves if we are going to have a chance at having a happy life. Our choices and decisions are usually based on the knowledge we have about ourselves and the outside world. If we let the outside world define for us who and what we are, then we are more likely to make choices which will not allow us to flourish as human beings can and should flourish.

CHAPTER THIRTEEN

The Pursuit of Happiness

In addition to correctly understanding what happiness is and knowing ourselves and the realities outside of ourselves, we must actively pursue and work for those things that will make us happy. Waiting for the lottery or any other reality outside of ourselves to make us happy will, with rare exceptions, not work (i.e., people have a greater chance of being hit by lightning and dying than they have of winning the lottery). We have to consciously and actively work for those things that we think will make us happy as described previously.

That doesn't mean that we can have control over everything in our lives. It is presumptuous to think or expect things to go our way because we want them to do so. There are too many variables that we cannot control. But we can't sit back and just react to life's events and encounters, hoping that good things will come our way.

Happiness is a lifelong work. It is always a work in progress. In many ways, I look at happiness as similar to constructing a strong building that will withstand the ever-changing and extremes of weather and the environment. I also look at it as doing the necessary maintenance of, and the re-investment/upgrades to, the building so that it lasts a long time and has rooms added to it as necessary and desired.

Happiness must be based on a strong foundation. That strong foundation consists, first, of our ideas of how we understand ourselves and the realities outside of ourselves; and second, our pro-active efforts to achieve those things that we think will make us truly happy.

If, from a career standpoint as an example, we think that being an accountant will make us happy as far as our work life is concerned, we have to prepare ourselves to do that work. We need the appropriate education and training. To move up in the profession, we need to get additional academic and professional training. The same goes for anything we want to pursue from a career standpoint as well as from our interactions with other outside interests and avocations. Most of us know this and are taught this.

What we are seldom taught is that the same kind of planning and execution is required to achieve happiness in other parts of our life as well; the more profound and deeply satisfying parts of our lives.

Just about everyone wants to love and be loved. If we want to be in a loving relationship with someone, we have to know what that loving relationship should consist of. Is it simply meeting someone, having a good time, and maybe having a sexual relationship with that person? Or, in order to pursue and attain the goal of a loving relationship, do we need also to seek a more in-depth, person-to-person relationship with that person? Do we need and want to understand that person as he or she truly is? Do we want to encounter that person in a way that is positive for both of us? If so, then we need to plan a course of action and related behaviors that help the loving relationship start. And then we need a plan and a course of action and behaviors that maintain and develop that relationship for the short run and the long run.

Too many loving relationships fail because people don't know what they are aiming for. When two people fall in love, they think it is sufficient for them as a human being to enjoy someone else's company and have a sexual relationship with them. Both elements are important and both can bring a certain amount of happiness to each. But human beings want more than that and they are not happy in the long run if they do not have more than that.

Two people need to understand that it takes more than liking another person and enjoying a sexual relationship with each other to have a happiness producing, long-term loving relationship between them. They need to understand that as a human being, as described previously, it is essential that the two people have a deeper bond and connection between themselves. It is a bond based on mutual knowledge of each other, trust, respect, openness, communication, and a shared vision of the future. It is based on truly desiring and choosing to do what is good for the other person. It is based on achieving the "I-Thou" relationship which I talked about earlier.

A firm foundation for a happiness producing, long-term, loving relationship requires the strong, interpersonal, loving relationship described above and in previous chapters.

And once that bond is created, it needs to be nourished and cultivated. Many people, when they fall in love, have elements of that deep, personal bond and connection. It is what most people experience as "falling in love," and which is also an important part of being drawn to another person. That close connection will sustain itself for awhile on its own momentum. But it will not continue to exist, or, more importantly, grow and deepen, unless both people actively pursue that goal by their on-going, conscious decisions, choices and behaviors. Once that deep connection and bond wanes and is eventually lost because of a lack of attention and effort, then the other two elements, enjoying each other's company and the sexual relationship, also deteriorate. And then people look for another relationship to provide that same joy and excitement that they first experienced and then lost in their previous relationship.

Building a happy life also requires us to make conscious choices about many things on an on-going basis. Very importantly, we have to make conscious choices to balance our time and attention to a variety of elements of our life. We need to balance our personal physical and mental health and well-being needs with those of our interpersonal relationships, our work life, and our leisure time. We need to balance our needs as material/physical beings with our spiritual needs. Too much emphasis and time spent in any area is generally not healthy and happiness producing. That doesn't mean we have to have a daily or weekly plan worked out for ourselves so that we are balancing our time and energy on all of the elements which are happiness producing. But it does mean that we have to order our life so that all of those elements get attention on a regular basis. And, we need to stop and examine our life from time to time to see if we are devoting sufficient time and attention to the different elements.

Sometimes realties in the world around us require us to focus our efforts so strongly in one area that the other areas can suffer. There are times in our work lives when we just have to spend an enormous amount of time and energy to stay employed and achieve professional goals. And achieving those goals, whether they are financial, career progression, power, intellectual growth, scientific inquiry and discovery, etc., can bring us a lot of happiness. But if they are achieved at the expense of our loving relationships, or our physical and/or metal health, or our spiritual life, then they are not happiness producing for the long run.

Illness, war, natural catastrophes, unemployment, and many other outside forces can require us to focus our efforts in one area of our lives. These are not things we would choose to deal with, but they occur for most of us some times in our lives. During these times it is difficult to maintain a balance and we may not be able to do so for some period of time. The danger when these events occur is not only that we suffer physical and/or mental injury, but that we also lose the balance of good things that we want and need in our lives.

Hard times are part of life. We can be happy through hard times if we have a good understanding of who and what we are, and where we are going, and we have a firm foundation of loving relationships in our lives. That doesn't mean that we don't feel the pain. It just means that we will have a better chance of getting through it because we have a good foundation of loving relationships to support us and we have a set of ultimate goals that make sense to us and give us hope.

In summary, I don't expect that the discussion of happiness set forth above covers the topic broadly enough or will answer every question that people have about living a happy life. But I think the three elements that are set forth below and which I discussed above are a good basis for thinking about living a happy life.

1.   We have to define happiness.
2.   We have to know ourselves and the world of realities outside of ourselves.
3.   We must actively pursue and work for those things that will make us happy.

Within this framework of thought and actions, I think we have the best chance of having a happy life. I have met and gotten to know many people over the years. In my experience, those who generally are unhappy are unhappy because:

- They are aiming for the wrong things to make them happy.
- They are aiming for the wrong things because they do not know themselves and the world around them very well.
- They expect good things to happen to them without planning for and working for them.

Finding our way through the complexities of our inner/personal world and the broader world with which we interact constantly is a challenging task. And it is complex. There are no easy answers. We have to be able to live with ambiguity and uncertainty. We never know ourselves completely any more than we know everything we need to know about the realities outside of ourselves with which we interact, including another person. And despite our best plans and intentions, we do not always accomplish or attain the good things we work for in our life to make us happy. But it is better to have a thoughtful and action-oriented framework within which to pursue happiness than to let things just happen to us or to pursue things that others say will make us happy, but often don't.

CHAPTER FOURTEEN

Truth, Goodness, and Beauty Defined

There is one other important set of elements that I think is very important when talking about "How should I live my life in order to be happy?" These elements are the closely intertwined concepts of Truth, Goodness, and Beauty.

Truth, Goodness, and Beauty are concepts and realities that only human beings can seek, be in relationship to, and enjoy. Because that ability is unique to human beings, it is important that we understand these terms and consciously seek all three. As I said before, I think one of the most important elements in living a happy life is to choose to do those things that are unique to who and what we are as human beings.

Again, and like most topics in this book, bookshelves are filled with books about truth, beauty, and goodness. I am not going to cover every aspect of the three terms because that is impossible in a short essay and I am not learned enough to presume to do so. But I would like to ask and answer three questions that I think are important to living a happy life:

- What do the terms Truth, Goodness, and Beauty mean?
- What does it mean to seek and be in relationship to Truth, Goodness, and Beauty?
- How does seeking and being in relationship to Truth, Goodness, and Beauty relate to happiness?

What is Truth?

Truth is knowledge that we possess which accurately and completely reflects the realities of any entity which exists.

For example, it is the Truth to say that I exist. What that existence consists of and means is open to interpretation. But the Truth that I exist is not open to interpretation. My knowledge of my existence accurately and completely reflects the realities that actually exist. It is the truth to say that I exist.

It is also the Truth when I say that I am sitting at my computer at this moment typing this sentence. The truthfulness of many other sentences I have written in this book may be true or not true depending on how close my words and ideas come to accurately and completely reflecting the realities about which I have written. But it is a definite Truth to say that as I write this sentence, I am writing this sentence.

Some people say that there is no Truth. They say that Truth is completely relative, and everything we know and say about anything is just our own perception and interpretation of reality. I disagree. I think the two simple examples above clearly show that we do know the Truth about some things. But I do agree that what we know about many things is not the whole Truth. We know parts of the Truth. We need to recognize that in many things, particularly the more complex matters, that each of us only knows part of the Truth.

Determining Truth is much more difficult and elusive as the realities we are trying to know become more complex. Knowing the truth about social, economic, political, historical, literary, philosophical, theological and a whole range of other bodies of knowledge and topics is a much more difficult task. Most of us think we know the truth about some of these things. But the Truth is, each of us has only has a partial understanding of the true reality of these things.

An example of the complexities of knowing the full Truth about any complex thing is the following words from the Declaration of Independence of the United States of America:

"We hold these truths to be self-evident, that all men are created equal, that they are endowed by their Creator with certain unalienable Rights, that among these are Life, Liberty and the pursuit of Happiness."

Are these truths self-evident? Do we all agree that they are self-evident? Do we all agree what the terms mean? Do the terms mean the same today as 200-plus years ago?

Are all men created equal? In what sense are they created equal? In what ways are they not created equal? Does this statement apply to women as well? How about slaves who are African Americans?

Who is this Creator? How do we know that a Creator exists? What does that term mean if we do not think there is a Creator?

Are Life, Liberty and the pursuit of Happiness really inalienable rights? If so, why did so many people throughout history, and many yet today, not enjoy these rights, or even be aware of them as Rights? What does Liberty mean? Does it mean that all people have the Liberty to meet and self-determine what they want their government to be? Or, does it mean I can do anything I want as an individual? What does the Right to Life mean? Does a zygote or fetus have a Right to Life?

The point is that even things we generally take to be Truths are often open to interpretation by many and even rejection by some. Also, as discussed extensively in an earlier chapter, how many Truths which we think are self evident are really beliefs?

I defined Truth as knowledge that we possess that accurately and completely reflect the realities of anything that exists. The bottom line about knowing the Truth is that we should recognize two things when trying to know the Truth about things, particularly complex things. First, we need to know that the reality of any particular thing (person, event, historical happening, physical entity, etc.) actually exists as it really is, independent of what we may think or want it to be. And, second, in most cases, we will only partially possess the Truth of that reality. It doesn't mean the Truth isn't out there. It only means that most of the time, for most things, we will only know part of the Truth.

So, we must always be learning about most things because it gives us a better chance to understand the realities which we encounter. If we possess knowledge that is as close to the Truth as possible, then we at least have a chance of making decisions and choices that will have the best results for us as individuals and for society as a whole.

What is Goodness?

Goodness is a quality which an entity (person, place, thing, idea, etc.) possesses when that entity contains or is made up of all the elements that fully make it what it is without any essential defect.

For example, a good apple is one that possesses all of the elements that an apple should contain (various physical, chemical and biological constituents) as well as a number of elements (size, color, ripeness, aroma, crunchiness, taste, etc.) that an apple should possess when an apple is fully what it is.

An apple that is rotting, or is filled with worms, or is half eaten and thrown in a garbage can, or maybe is injected with a magic potion like the evil witch did in "Snow White and the Seven Dwarfs," is not considered a good apple. It's a bad apple! A bad apple contains many of the elements that an apple should have, but it has some elements which are either missing, or added, or are less than fully developed.

For another simple example, if we say we have a bad leg, it usually means that all of the leg parts are there, but something is not at its best. Maybe we have sprained the leg. Maybe we have broken it. Maybe gangrene has set in and we are going to lose the leg.

Like Truth, I think Goodness does exist as an objective reality outside of ourselves. Certainly, there can be differences of opinion about what constitutes the goodness of an apple or a leg. But most of the time most of us can agree that some things possess goodness and some do not.

The above definition of goodness may seem a bit strange and over-wrought, but I think it captures the essence of what goodness is. And, I think it is important to define what goodness is in order to know what we should be seeking when we make decisions and choices about what is good for us and for society as a whole.

That is why I spent a lot of time earlier in this book talking about what reality is in general, and what reality is as far as what constitutes a human being. We can only be a good human being and live a good life, if we know as best as possible what it means to be a human being and then what it means to be the best of what a human being is.

If we don't understand what a human being really is, I think we will have a greater tendency to make decisions that are not good for us and/or others. For instance, making enough money to live a life that meets our needs as a human being is good. Making enough money to pursue activities and things that give us the opportunity to live more fully and flourish as human beings is even a greater good. But thinking that making lots of money will make us happy in and of itself is not a good decision for ourselves and others. We should understand that making lots of money, in and of itself, will not make us happy. Certainly winning the lottery gives the winner a certain sense of euphoria. But how many lottery winners, after several years, turned out to not be very happy people? They probably were not happy people before they won the lottery and they were not very happy after a relatively brief period of excitement and good feeling after they won the money. As a manager of many people, I have seen people get raises and bonuses that made them happy for a short time. And that is good. But once their basic monetary needs are met, people are happy at their work if they have a chance to flourish as a human being and as a valued and productive person.

Money can certainly give us the opportunity to acquire and do things that might make us happy. But the happiness we will experience over the long run will be tied more directly to meeting the needs of who and what we truly are as described earlier. We will be happy and live a good life if we are the best of what a human being can be in general, and the best of what we can be as a specific human being.

What is Beauty?

What do you think of when someone asks you what is beautiful?

I think of several things right off the bat: a beautiful woman; a beautiful sunset; a beautiful aria by Puccini sung by Pavarotti; a beautiful scientific theory; a beautiful person; a beautiful landscape; a beautiful flower; a beautiful friendship. The list can go on and on.

So the question is, "What makes these things beautiful?"

My answer is that Beauty is the optimal harmony of the constituent parts of an entity.

Everything is made up of many elements. When those elements blend together at their highest level, we describe that entity as beautiful.

Beauty is something that an entity possesses whether we see that entity or not. The old saying is that "Beauty is in the eye of the beholder." Certainly the eye can behold Beauty. But Beauty exists in something whether we as an individual behold it or not.

One very interesting thing about Beauty is that it isn't always tied to physical or material reality. We are able to perceive Beauty in many things that are not material in any way. For example, I always loved the idea that one of the tests of whether or not a scientist is on the right track in developing a theory is when the theory becomes beautiful. What the scientist usually means when she says that is everything comes together perfectly in the theory. It answers many questions in a cohesive and integrated way. And hence, the theory is beautiful!

Another example is to say that a friendship is beautiful. Again, there are many constituent elements that make up a beautiful friendship. Some of the elements are material and physical in nature and some are the non-material personal relationship and bond that exists between two friends.

I also find it interesting that Beauty is often associated with artistic work of various kinds. Why is Michelangelo's "David" a beautiful sculpture? Why is the ceiling of the Sistine Chapel considered a beautiful painting? Why is the Viet Nam Memorial Wall in Washington D.C. considered a beautiful work of architecture?

I think most people consider the above works of art to be beautiful because they capture both the physical/material elements of an entity as well as the spiritual/non-material elements of an entity. The elements are all combined into a wonderful harmony of the material and non-material. Certainly they are all portrayed in a material way. But they are beautiful, because they capture the harmony, the convergence of both the material and the non-material aspects of reality.

Often artistic works of all types go beyond the mere representational. They create and reflect a reality which goes beyond the material. They creatively blend and harmonize many elements into a coherent and beautiful whole. We find them beautiful because they reach us at the deepest parts of who we are - material and spiritual beings.

To summarize:

Truth is knowledge that we possess that accurately and completely reflects the realities of any entity which exists.

Goodness is a quality which an entity possesses when that entity contains, or is made up of, all the elements that fully make it what it is without any essential defect.

Beauty is the optimal harmony of the constituent parts of an entity.

CHAPTER FIFTEEN

Truth, Goodness, and Beauty in Relationship to Happiness

Since Truth, Goodness, and Beauty are concepts that only human beings can seek, be in relationship to and enjoy, how do we as human beings relate to these three realities?

Some say that we possess these items. They say it is the goal of human beings is to possess Truth, Goodness, and Beauty. To a certain degree, I agree with them. We do want to possess these things.

But I think that as much as we want to possess Truth, Goodness, and Beauty, we also want to be in relationship to them.

In some ways, we possess the Truth because what we know becomes part of who we are. But we also want to be functioning in a reality that is real and True. One reason we all hate to be lied to is that we find out that the reality we thought we were encountering and living in relationship to is not true.

In some ways we possess Goodness in the sense that we have things about ourselves that are good: our health, our talents, our intellect, maybe our good looks. Also, we want to possess things that are outside of ourselves that we perceive to be good in themselves and would be good for us if we possessed them. The whole world of advertising and consumption is based on our desire as human beings to possess good things that are outside of ourselves and/or will make us better, happier people if we possess them. But besides possessing the good, we also want to live in a reality where we are in relationship to good things, especially good people. We are drawn to good people like moths to a flame. We want to be in their presence. That is why celebrity is such a phenomenon of our time. Many people are thrilled to be in the presence of celebrities because they are presented to us as being good and desirable people. Unfortunately, they often turn out to not be as good as real people as they are portrayed or we hope they are. But there is no question that we want to be in the presence of good people and good things.

Like Truth and Goodness, we also possess Beauty to some degree. Certainly a model with a beautiful face and body possesses Beauty. Some people possess a Beauty of soul and spirit. Some people possess a beautiful mind or heart. But more than anything, most of our experiences of Beauty are in relationship to beautiful things outside of ourselves. We encounter Beauty all of the time. Unfortunately, we don't always recognize it or take the time to encounter it. Like Goodness, Beauty draws us to itself. We are pulled out of ourselves when we encounter the Beautiful. We become more alive and more complete as a human being when we encounter Beauty. That is why we want to be in the presence of Beauty.

Finally, I think it is interesting that Truth, Goodness, and Beauty, are tied closely together. Knowing the Truth is Good. Things that are True and Good are often very beautiful. Keats said, "Beauty is truth, truth beauty, that is all ye know on earth and all ye need to know." I always liked that line because it captures the inter-relatedness of Truth and Beauty. My own addition is that what is True and Beautiful is also Good!

How does seeking and being in relationship to Truth, Goodness, and Beauty relate to happiness?

The bottom line to me is that if we pursue Truth, Goodness, and Beauty, we will be living our lives in ways that are in line with what and who we are as human beings. We will flourish if we pursue, possess, and are in the presence of all three as often as we can throughout our lives.

Pursuing all three takes time. Sometimes we succeed in finding the Truth and sometimes we fail. Sometimes we get pretty close to the Truth in complex situations. Sometimes we stubbornly cling to our previous understanding of reality and refuse to change our minds when presented with new information. The closer we can get to the Truth, the better chance we have of making good decisions and choices which affect our happiness, and often the happiness of others.

Sometimes we find the real Good. Very often, we are misled as to what is the Good. We all want the Good for ourselves and often for others. But discerning the real Good takes thought and knowledge of the realities outside of ourselves and inside of ourselves. Good things are things that help us truly flourish as human beings. False Goods sometimes provide us with short-time feelings of happiness, but in the long run, they do not satisfy us and often they can hurt us and those around us. As an extreme example, the next snort of cocaine looks like a Good to a junkie, but the result of the attainment of that Good is self-destruction.

Finding Beauty above all takes time and attention. Sometimes we are overwhelmed by the Beautiful and just stop to be in its presence, to admire it, and to enjoy it. But most of the time, we are too busy with all kinds of activities, or distracted by too much "noise" of all kinds, or too busy acquiring things to notice and appreciate the beautiful.

I am not saying that we have to constantly stop and think about pursuing the True, the Good, and the Beautiful. But if we think those three aspects of reality are important to living a good and happy life, we will take some time, and even make some time, when we can think about what is really True, Good, and Beautiful about reality in and outside of ourselves, and pursue them as we encounter reality as whole.

If we pursue the Truth, we will be in better touch with reality and we will make better decisions and choices.

If we pursue the Good, we will flourish more as human beings and be happier.

If we pursue the Beautiful, we will also flourish as human beings, we will have a greater understanding of what is True, and we will be lifted out of ourselves to a higher level of being.

CHAPTER SIXTEEN

Evil

Evil exists. We all have to deal with it as human beings.

Even though there is truth, goodness, beauty, and love as part of reality, their opposites of falsehood, badness, ugliness, and hate, also exist.

Evil is basically something that harms ourselves or another entity. And, we define harm to be something which damages the completeness, wholeness, and/or flourishing of any entity.

Evil comes at us from outside of ourselves. It also can come from within ourselves.

Like truth, goodness, and beauty, we live in relationship to evil. We need to understand it so that we can make decisions and choices which will help ourselves, others, and the world around us to flourish.

Evil is usually easy to recognize, but is hard to define. One way to start defining evil is to think about it as falling into two categories:

-Natural events.

-Human decisions and actions.

Natural Events are those processes of nature that affect everything in the universe. Most natural processes are not evil. But the result of some natural processes causes evil for us as human beings. An earthquake, in and of itself, is not evil. If it kills my children and destroys my home, it is evil. The birth and death of plant and animal life is not evil. It is just the natural process or cycle of life. Our own death to us, and maybe some family members and friends, is an evil;

but to the rest of the universe, it is just a natural process to which all of life, human and otherwise, is subject. In relationship to the evil associated with natural processes, we try to avoid them, prepare for them to minimize the evil consequences to us as humans, and/or try to mitigate the harm that is done to us as humans as a result of the natural process.

It is important to note that the evil associated with natural catastrophes and processes is the result of how those events and processes affect us as human beings either individually or collectively. Evil is a human concept and experience. It is something we as humans can experience because we have the capacity to be self-consciously aware of and assess the harm that is being done to us. For example, if a giant raptor swoops down out of the sky, scoops me up by the scruff of my neck, and then takes me to her nest where I am killed and fed to her baby raptors, most people would consider that to be an evil to me as a particular human being. If that same raptor swooped down and picked up a rabbit, killed it, and fed it to the baby raptors, most people would not consider that an evil. It is just part of reality and the natural cycle of life. In both instances, what the raptor is doing in and of itself is not evil. In fact, it is a good thing for a raptor to provide food for its babies. But as a human being, I consider the raptor's action evil when she grabs me, or grabs you for that matter, for the family meal. But I don't consider it an evil when the raptor grabs the rabbit for dinner.

Sickness and death are natural things that affect us as human beings. Both are evil or bad things when they affect us or anyone we know and love. Nobody wants to suffer illness and die. As human beings, we try to avoid and mitigate illness and its attendant suffering. We cannot avoid death. Death is evil in the sense that our life as we know it will be ended. If this life is all there is, then death is the ultimate evil to each of us personally. If there is more to life than what we currently experience, then death is a passage to another type of life.

I think death is a natural part of life and that when we die, we move on to another type of existence. I may be wrong. Whether I am right or wrong, death is a part of the natural order. I don't think I have anything to lose by thinking and believing that my existence will continue. In fact, as discussed elsewhere, I think it is a more credible belief on my part than the belief that I will go out of existence when I die.

Human Decisions and Actions are the other source of evil in our lives. As human beings, we have the capacity to make decisions and take actions which are good or evil. The basic criteria for whether or not one of our decisions and actions is good or evil is whether or not harm is done to some aspect of reality.

We all are the source of evil to ourselves, to others, or to any aspect of reality outside of ourselves. We make decisions and take actions which result in evil because of two reasons. First, we do not have a clear understanding of what the reality of something is so we think we are choosing something good, when in actuality we are causing harm. Second, we intentionally choose to inflict harm on others.

Because of a lack of understanding and knowledge, we may make a decision and take an action which causes harm to ourselves or any other entity. Such acts may not be intentionally evil. We may not really choose that harm come to ourselves or other entities based on our decisions and actions. In fact, many decisions we make and actions we take are done on the basis that we think it is good for ourselves or for others. But whether or not we intentionally choose to act in a way that causes harm to ourselves or others, if the action harms ourselves or any other entity, we are the source of that evil.

That is why I have been so strongly emphasizing the importance of knowing reality as best we can. The more we actually know of reality, the better chance we have of not inflicting harm through ignorance. If we think that the main purpose of life is to be rich, famous or powerful, then we will make decisions and take actions that will achieve that goal no matter what the consequences are to ourselves or others. We will harm ourselves because an overemphasis on achieving wealth, celebrity or power will not help us fully flourish as a human being as described earlier. Also, in making choices and taking actions to maximize our wealth, our fame, or our power, we will frequently achieve those goals at the expense of, and harm to, other individuals and entities. We may not always see the harm that will come to us or other entities, but damage to ourselves and/or other entities does occur. Sometimes, we may think we are actually doing something good, like starting a war to protect our interests, whereas in reality, we inflict harm on ourselves as well as those whom we consider our enemies.

The second instance of inflicting harm on ourselves or others is when we intentionally choose to do so. The junkie taking another snort of cocaine is certainly hurting himself. He is probably aware, some of the time at least, that he is hurting himself by continuing to use the drug. He may be too addicted at some point to be able to control his desire to have another snort. But somewhere in the chain of events from taking the first snort to getting to the point of total self-destruction, the junkie made some choices that have resulted in his current condition.

Hurting others is, unfortunately, a very common thing we do as human beings. We do it by words and by actions. Often we do it in retaliation for a real or imagined harm that was done to us. We all have the capacity as human beings to make such decisions and take such harmful actions. Human beings are the only entities that can deliberately make such decisions and take such actions. And all of us, to some extent, have knowingly and deliberately made decisions and taken actions to cause harm to others. None of us is without fault. It is part of who and what we are as human beings as we discussed earlier.

Living in Relationship to Evil

We can choose the true, the good, and the beautiful. But we are also just as capable of choosing the false, the bad, and the ugly. And what we can do as individuals as far as choosing and taking actions that result in evil, we are also capable of doing as a society. Current news stories and the historical record show the incredible and horrific capacity and ability that human beings have to inflict violence, pain, suffering, and death on other human beings.

We need to be vigilant in making individual and societal decisions so that we choose good over evil. We must know the realities of ourselves and situations so that we do not choose a course of action that results in harm based on ignorance or based on malice. We must not take for granted that as individuals or as a society that we will know what is the good thing to do; or that even knowing what the good thing to do is, that we will choose it.

The difference between what is good and what is evil is not just a matter of interpretation. Some choices and actions are good and some are evil. My answer to people who say that good and evil is a

matter of interpretation is that in some cases it is, but in some cases
the distinction is very clear. If I disagree with your assessment of a
situation and the consequent course of action to take, I can understand that. Maybe you have better information than me. Maybe you
are a better person than me. On the other hand, maybe I am more
correct in my assessment of the situation and my course of action will
have a better result than yours. I can live with that difference. But,
if as a result of that difference of understanding, I pick up a baseball
bat and bash your brains in until you are dead, that is wrong. That is
an evil. I don't think anyone would disagree with the evilness of that
action, particularly the person whose head is bashed in.

There are many things that almost all people agree are evil:
child sexual abuse, murdering an innocent person, animal torture,
eating a sumptuous meal amid a group of starving people, etc. The
list is quite extensive.

There are also many things that some people see as evil and others do not: abortion, birth control, sexual relationships outside of
marriage, homosexual relationships, unequal distribution of income,
starting a preemptive war… Again, the list is quite extensive.

Often, when people see different things as evils or goods, the
differing views are based on different ideologies and/or theologies.
People on both sides of the issue bring very different sets of assump-
tions and facts to the discussion. Usually, the argument is not about
the intrinsic nature of the action, but about how the action or issue
fits into the worldview created by the ideology or theology of the parties to the disagreement.

I am not totally opposed to ideologies and theologies. We need
frameworks within which we make moral and ethical decisions.
We don't have the time or knowledge to carefully examine the pros
and cons of every moral decision that confronts us. But what I am

saying is that when there are people of good will and who live good lives on both sides of a moral question, there is usually some truth in both sides of the argument. As an individual, I have the right and duty to choose the good as I see it in my own personal decisions. But in a civil society, I do not think it is appropriate to force my ideological and theological certainties onto others any more than they should do so to me. I can persuade people and try to get a majority of my elected officials to enact laws which represent my views. But that is different than coercing and intimidating people to accept and follow my views.

Many of the evils described above are about significant and major issues. Most of us agree that most of those things are evils. When confronted with decisions in these areas, we are more likely to think about the good and evil aspects of them. But most of us for most of our lives are not confronted with those major decisions on big issues. The evil that most of us indulge in or succumb to are the smaller, on-going behaviors that have a corrosive and damaging affect on ourselves and/or on those with whom we interact regularly. The most important area where we do our most damage is in our interpersonal relationships with people we want to love or supposedly love. The mean word, the not-so-subtle put down, the lack of respect for the other person's individuality, the power relationships which are claimed and enforced, and the inattention to the other person's needs is where we do the most damage. We create a climate of disrespect and hostility. It affects our own relationships and the relationships of others with us; and, when done in a broader social context of family or society as a whole, it introduces anger, mistrust, falsehood and hate into the broader realities with which we all have to deal.

Spreading falsehoods, exerting dominance and coercion over individuals and groups, promoting and indulging in bigotry, being greedy, and spreading hate are much worse wrongs than the evils associated with sexual behaviors between two consenting adults. I am not saying that all behaviors associated with sexual activity are good. In fact, they are evil when there is an aspect of abuse associated with those behaviors. But the evils brought about by hatred, bigotry, violence, etc. are much more serious and do much more damage in most cases than those brought about by "sins of the flesh."

Finally, choosing between good and evil is not just a matter of how we feel about something. Our feelings can be a help to us in deciding many things. If we feel good about something, we will want to choose it and pursue it, and vice-versa. But the fact that we feel good about some decision or that we think doing something will make us feel good, that is not enough to guarantee that we are choosing good over evil.

The bottom line is that some things are truly good and some are truly evil. And there are a lot of gray areas in between. Like searching for truth, we will seldom attain the total truth of a situation and we will seldom know absolutely what is the good decision and action to take. But that does not mean that we should go through life not looking for and choosing the good. If we don't, we are led or pushed by others who want us to follow what they determine to be good for us, and often and not incidentally, what is good for them.

Evil and God

How can there be a God when there is so much evil in the world? How can God let a child get cancer and die? How can God allow a tsunami to wipe out hundreds of thousands of lives? How can God allow the Holocaust?

Those and many similar questions are reasons that people have told me over the years as the reason why they don't believe in God; or if there is a God, people say he can't be a very good God because he allows or causes such terrible things to happen. Those are certainly legitimate questions.

I think that the main problem with reconciling evil with God is that our traditional language and imagery about God does not allow us to do so. Earlier in this book I spoke about the dominant imagery of an all-powerful God who controls everything. That is a human projection of who and what God is based on scriptures that were written two to three thousand years ago by men who lived in a patriarchal, hierarchical, and juridical world. Their stories and images of God reflected that cultural environment. That language and those images are too limiting of who and what God is.

More recent theologians have at least broadened our language about a God who creates but does not control. They also give us language and images of a relational God who created the world, moves our minds, hearts, and spirits to do good things, but does not dominate the direction and decisions that human beings make. Also, newer theological discussion gives us language and images of God as infusing and drawing all of humanity to a closer and ultimate relationship with God. Others talk about us co-creating with God the future of humanity and the entire world we live in.

Before human beings came on the scene (whether through creation or evolution), there was no evil in the sense that I discussed above. Everything was just the natural processes of living and dying, becoming and ending, ever evolving into a rich tapestry of all types of animate and inanimate entities. Evil, in regards to the natural processes of reality, came into being when human beings became aware of their own pain, suffering, and ultimate death. We began to call some things evil. Before that, evil did not exist. And, unfortunately, evil became more of a reality when we human beings started doing evil things to ourselves and to each other.

We are beings with a free will to choose and we too often choose what is evil and harmful to ourselves and others. That is our problem as human beings. That is not God's fault.

So, I do not see God as the source or cause of evil. We, as human beings, created the concept of evil in regards to how natural processes negatively affect us as human beings. And as human beings, we perform evil acts that harm ourselves and other aspects of reality.

Evil and Sin

Sin is a theological concept. It is generally defined as an evil act which offends God and which harms ourselves or any other aspect of reality.

When talking about sin, the emphasis is most often on the "offending God" portion of the definition. Not as much attention is paid to the second part of the definition: the evil that all of us do which brings harm to ourselves and other aspects of reality, including other people.

All of the earliest records of any group of people anywhere in the world contain stories of offending and appeasing the Gods. That language and those concepts reflected hierarchical and legal cultures and environments of those times. And they have persisted through history. Many people today still believe in a God who judges our actions and will reward or punish us based on those actions.

In the last 100 years or so, a combination of a diminishing belief in God as well as the rise of the many therapeutic social and medical sciences have caused the idea of sin to fall out of common parlance. Certainly, if there is no God, then there is no sin in the traditional sense. Unfortunately for some, the next step in the reasoning process is to say that since there is no God and there is no sin, then there is no right or wrong. Anything that someone does that is considered wrong or evil is explained by the combination of nature and nurture which determined the person's choice and consequent actions. So a person who does something that does harm to themselves or others, or any part of, reality is just choosing among things that appeal to them or really has no choice about what they are choosing. Choices are all genetically determined. We just have the illusion of choosing.

If someone does not believe in God that does not mean that there is no right or wrong. It means that there is no God to offend, so there is no sin in the traditional sense. But whether or not we believe in God, there is still a right or wrong. And, it is still our responsibility, and what is best for us and other elements of reality, to choose the good over the evil, the right over the wrong.

If we do believe in God, as I do, I think there is too much emphasis about offending God. Again, we apply human terms and concepts to our understanding of God. Those terms are too limiting of Who and What God is. I guess it is possible to offend God, though how some mere mortal like myself among billions of mortals now and more billions in the past could really offend God seems like a strange concept to me?

The emphasis should really be on the choices we make that either help or hurt our development as individuals, as a society, and the total physical reality as discussed previously. Deliberately polluting a lake with mercury from which people catch and eat fish is wrong. It is a sin if you believe in God. But whether or not you believe in God, it is wrong. To sexually abuse a child is a sin if you believe in God. But again, whether or not you believe in God, it is wrong.

Our role as human beings, as I have described from various perspectives previously, is to fully participate in the realities we interact with in a positive and life-affirming manner. We are to co-create a better world that allows and fosters all of reality to flourish as best as it can. Things we do that are contrary to that role are detrimental to us as individuals and to reality as a whole. It doesn't make any difference to me if we consider our evil acts as sins. That is just a term. The real issue is whether or not we are living as a human being is capable of living, not only in terms of what is good for me, but what is good for the entire reality which I am in relationship to and interact with.

CHAPTER SEVENTEEN

Happiness and the God Factor

"Anxiety or sickness unto death," is a phrase I read and internalized many years ago. I don't recall if Sartre or Camus used those terms or even that phraseology. But from the context in which I read it, what stuck with me is that the author was trying to convey to his readers that one of the central problems of being a human being is that we are all aware that we will die. We are the only creatures we know of who know that they will die. We are also the only creatures who are self-aware enough to think about the possibility that when we die, we will also cease to exist in any manner or as any other type of being whatsoever. Camus and/or Sartre are saying that as a result of that underlying fear of our own possible, total non-existence, we experience a deep anxiety. And, that deep anxiety is one of the most dominant, underlying emotional states that all human beings live with and try to cope with.

Because of that knowledge and a related sense of doom and anxiety, human beings are constantly looking for things that relieve that anxiety and sense of foreboding. Most people try many things to ease that anxiety or suppress it entirely. From an individual standpoint, people procreate to gain a certain sense of immortality. They try to achieve wealth or power or fame. They try to control the circumstances of their lives. They try to minimize the dangers and threats that confront them from realities outside of themselves.

A few people proudly assert that their fatalistic acceptance of their ultimate nothingness is what strong people do. If they don't say it outright, they at least imply that the rest of us weaklings invent God and eternal life to save ourselves from this anxiety. And in one sense they are correct. Most of us as individuals and groups over millennia have created gods and religions to help us cope with the challenges of life as a human being.

But also, human beings have created many other philosophies and societal structures to cope with this sense of anxiety and the desire to understand reality in ways which will help us be happy and successful as individuals and as societies. We have also created what the Bible and other long-lived religious texts and traditions call false gods. Money, power, and unfettered/unlimited sexual relationships are some of the things we are told to pursue in life as things that will make us happy and safe; or at least will help us enjoy our limited time of existence to its utmost.

On the intellectual side, we create a broad range of ideologies and theories about social and economic interactions and institutions which will, in turn, create a heaven on earth. Some of the ideologies from the current and recent past include communism, fascism, Nazism, scientism, capitalism, democracy, militarism, and nationalism. Most of these ideologies have some value. They all try to lessen our anxiety about the world we live in. They try to give us rational explanations of why we are afraid and anxious, and give us ideas and images to assuage that anxiety and fear. Just think of "the Invisible Hand" of Adam Smith. In economics, there is no god, but there is the Invisible Hand of the marketplace which makes everything work out for the best. And, if we just let this Invisible Hand work, we won't have any fears or anxieties.

Almost all of these ideologies have some value. Some have more value than others. They are of value because they explain some aspects of reality that we all encounter and then they lay out a basis of understanding these realities and a related societal structure in which they should operate. But no ideology is broad enough to encompass all of the complexities of the world in which we live. And that is why, over centuries sometimes, ideologies and societal structures rise and fall, and are eventually replaced by new theories and structures.

All I am saying is that we as human beings are anxious at our core because we fear the end of our existence and our eventual nothingness. And because of that fear and anxiety, we create ideologies and structures that help us cope with that.

The most basic of realities, as I have discussed previously in this book, is my rationally supported belief that God does exist. Based on that judgment, and the consequent judgment that human beings are spiritual/physical entities, I think that our spiritual beings will not go out of existence.

Because of that understanding of and belief in God and myself as a human being that will continue to exist, even after I physically die, I think the God Factor is important in living a happy life.

That doesn't mean that people can't experience a great deal of happiness in their lives without believing in God. But I think, in the hardest times of our lives, the times we face our own mortality, the times we are thoughtfully self-aware of ourselves, the times that we become anxious unto death; at that point, we can relieve that anxiety and fear by recognizing who and what we are as spiritual/physical entities and then pursue activities that are in concert with that self knowledge and awareness of our spiritual reality. Or, we can say it makes no difference and suppress those feelings of anxiety, and carry on with our lives bravely and pursue the tangible, material things that we think will make us happy.

But since the suppression of that anxiety is not addressed, it pops up in our lives in many ways. Rather than addressing the core issue of our anxiety, which is our fear of becoming nothingness, we project that fear and anxiety onto other aspects of our lives. We want to be protected from any and every real and imagined threat to ourselves.

From a group standpoint, we project our fears and anxieties onto others. Today those fears and anxieties are projected onto terrorists, Muslims, homosexuals, femi-nazis, and minorities of any kind. In the past, the list of enemies that threatened our individual and group well-being has included just about every group of people in the world. Christians used to kill Protestants and vice-versa. Frenchmen killed Germans and vice-versa. Athenians killed Spartans and vice-versa. Hutsis kill Tutsis and vice-versa. Arabs kill Jews and vice-versa. The list is endless.

From an individual standpoint, we worry about all kinds of things. Certainly, some things should be worried about. For example, the potential of losing a job for whatever reason is prudent. Taking steps to keep our job or prepare ourselves for a new job are actions that we take in response to our worries. But many things are not worth worrying about because they will not affect our happiness and well-being at the core of who we are as a human being. One current example of over-worrying is the almost hysterical fear for our children. Certainly parents need to be careful in raising their children. But it is almost ludicrous today the way parents are told to protect their babies. They are told to not put a blanket on a sleeping baby because they could suffocate. Mothers are told that they have to nurse their babies until they are least a year old or the babies will be scarred for life. Using baby talcum powder on a baby's diaper rash will cause them to get cancer someday. Get real!

Certainly intelligent beings such as humans, who have a basic survival instinct, should be prudently careful about things that might harm themselves, their families, and their society. But projecting fears and anxieties about our potential nothingness onto groups, individuals, and things outside of ourselves is counter-productive to living a happy life.

One thing I have tried to stress throughout these essays, and particularly as they relate to happiness, is that we all have a better chance of living a happier life if we live that life in harmony with the realities inside and outside of ourselves.

For the reasons set forth previously, I think and believe that God is the ultimate reality. We live and exist in relationship to God. We will be happiest if that awareness of the realities outside of ourselves is one of the guides to how we live our lives. It should not be the only reality which we take into account. But, I think, it should be one of them. Because without it, the underlying fear and anxiety of our eventual nothingness will never be addressed and we will look for a wide range of ineffectual and often harmful means to relieve that fear and anxiety.

CHAPTER EIGHTEEN

Religion, Spirituality, and Happiness

Religion is an attempt by human beings to translate their understanding of God into words and actions that they think are appropriate for themselves as interactive social beings.

Spirituality is our connection to the spiritual realities in us and outside of ourselves.

Spirituality is not religion. And, religion is not necessary for spirituality.

Religion can serve as an intellectual framework and set of guidelines for developing and practicing a spiritual life. But it is not a necessary condition or prerequisite for doing so.

Human beings are social beings. They naturally seek out the company of other human beings in almost everything they do. Some people seek more social interactions than others, but no human being can exist and flourish without interacting with other human beings to some degree.

It is not unexpected then that social beings, when trying to cope with the fundamental issues of what is reality and who and what we are, would form social structures and organizations to address such important matters. We do it for everything else in life from economics, to education, to entertainment. Why would we not do it for religion?

Religions are often based on sacred texts of some kind. Usually, the authors of the texts are considered to be inspired by God to write them; and, consequently, the texts are considered the Word of God.

These texts form the basis of the ideas about God for a particular religion as well as a code of behavior for the members of the religious group to follow.

Spirituality, on the other hand, is not something that necessarily needs a set of texts or a social structure in which to exist and flourish. Most of us, at the deepest core of who we are, experience ourselves as having a dimension which goes beyond mere physicality. We call this our spirit or soul. We can connect to that reality in ourselves, in other human beings, and with God without religion.

No particular religion has a lock on the reality of who or what God is. Most religions I have read about have some common concepts and practices. At the same time, they all differ in ways that are sometimes minor and sometimes significant.

The plus side of religion is that it can provide a framework of ideas and the lived experience and witness of many other human beings within which people as individuals and groups can regularize (a word that shares the same root with religion) their relationship with God and with other human beings, and flourish as human beings themselves. At its highest and most positive, religion can bring out the best in individuals and groups by setting high standards of behavior. It can give us the opportunity for individual and communal spiritual experiences with God and with each other that are joyful and hopeful. It can give us an altruistic rationale and a community/organizational structure to address the needs of those who most need our help. It can help us deal with some of the most difficult and challenging of life's experiences, including sickness and death. Very importantly, it can add to our knowledge base a practical, spiritual dimension to reality that we often fail to see if we are too caught up in the daily and often routine activities of living. Also, very importantly, it gives us the opportunities as individuals and groups to express and fulfill our human longing for encounters with God as Spirit.

The negative side of religion is that it is too often used as a control mechanism by people who want to get and then maintain power. Too often religion has been part of the political establishment and religion's doctrines and practices have been used to support political structures. Religion is too often used as a club or weapon to attack others with whom we disagree or by whom we feel threatened. Millions of people have been, and will continue to be, killed because of religion. But religion doesn't have a corner on killing others. Racial and ethnic genocides, as well as political systems and theories of all kinds (nationalism, communism, Nazism, imperialism, fascism, etc.), have all fomented and supported killing of others who are deemed to be different or a threat to the parties doing the killing.

Religion can also be used as an individual control mechanism over other individuals. Many religions have promoted and supported male dominance in interpersonal relationships. Some religions have supported slavery. Religion sometimes causes injury and pain to individuals themselves. It may cause them to think and feel that they are inadequate or damaged or condemned, or have an extraordinary amount of guilt to carry around. It may limit some of their behaviors in ways that are not in keeping with what is natural and healthy for a human being.

So religion is a very mixed bag. If looked at strictly from a social structure and set of ideas standpoint, religion is no better or worse than other ideologies and related structures that have come and gone over the years. And on that basis, there is no strong argument for being part of a religious group.

But, if looked at as an attempt to live and act in relationship to all of the realities out there, including God, then religion can give us a theological, philosophical, and practical framework in which to pursue those relationships.

I said earlier that the purpose of my life is to fully participate in the realities in which I exist.

I also said that happiness is the long-term state or condition of a human being who is in harmony with all of the realities in us and around us.

Since I think and believe that one of the realities of the world is that there is a God who we can describe as best we can as Spirit, then to be in touch with the reality of God, as best as we humans can, is to experience a type and level of happiness that I would not experience if I did not seek out such encounters. And for me, that can best be done by participating in religious rituals that give me an opportunity to encounter God as an individual and as part of a group, and studying/increasing my understanding of the divine and human spiritual dimensions of reality.

CHAPTER NINETEEN

Why I Am a Catholic

First, I was born and raised a Catholic. Without that experience, I am not sure I would be a Catholic today. But then, again, I might have become a Catholic even if I did not start out as one as C.S. Lewis, John Cardinal Newman, and many others have done.

I have examined many other faiths over the years. I have read about them and attended their religious ceremonies. I always found them wanting just as I have often found the Catholic Church wanting. Mostly, the other religions did not have the intellectual and theological depth to them that I was seeking. Often, they were overly individualistic and/or self-growth oriented. Some were way too condemnatory and/or controlling toward individuals and groups. Very importantly, they had a very limited focus on worshipping and being in relationship with God. A lot of the emphasis was on what going to church and praying can do for me...make me happier, gain God's favor and be richer, be a mental health and therapeutic experience, increase my self-esteem, etc. There was very little, if any, focus on the worship of God, simply because God is God and that God is worthy of worship and attention.

As I have written about earlier, I think it is important for us as human beings to be in harmony with all of the realities in us and around us. A human being, in order to be in harmony with the realities of God, needs to encounter God as the Creator and ultimate goal of life. Therefore, just as it is important to encounter individuals in our lives at our deepest levels of who and what we are as a person, it is just as important to devote time, energy, and effort to encountering God.

I sometimes think of encountering God in the same sense that I am drawn to and react with overwhelming awe to a beautiful sunset or mountain valley, or being in the presence of a beautiful work of art or beautiful music. When we encounter these things, we don't have to tell ourselves to be in awe. It just happens. We are drawn out of ourselves and experience reality at a more intense level. We are moved and touched by such experiences, and they stay with us and become part of who we are. Sometimes, we are fortunate enough to meet another human being who is truly awe-inspiring because of their goodness and accomplishments. Great leaders have this capacity to show us a vision and a way to get there. We follow because we want to be part of that goal and achievement. We become more than what we ordinarily think and feel ourselves to be.

So, I seek out encounters with God. And I have found that the Catholic religion and liturgies have given me the best opportunities to have those encounters.

The Catholic Church is certainly not perfect and not without its problems. In some aspects of its teachings and practice, it has been deplorable both in the present day and during its long history. I don't diminish or dismiss those realities. And over the years, I have tried to improve it as an organization and I have tried to participate within the limited opportunities I have had to change its teachings and practices as well.

But at the same time, in my experience, every organization I have ever participated in or read about has had its shortcomings and perpetrated a number of evils, including the Catholic Church.

And because of those shortcomings, I could abandon the Catholic Church.

But to me, the Catholic Church is more than its organizational structure and programs. It is more than its hierarchy and its priests. It is more than its many, many failures.

It is a people seeking God.

And, very importantly to me, the Catholic Church has the broadest, and deepest, and most human understanding of God that I have found. One of the things I like about any theory of anything is that it is comprehensive - that it takes into account the broadest array of information, answers the most questions, and sees connections between things that most people never see or often overlook. That is the case in scientific theories. Scientists know that they are on to something when the theory they are constructing integrates as much information as possible and answers as many questions as possible. As the theory comes together, scientists use the word "beautiful" to describe the theory. There is a simplicity and harmony between all of the parts that makes the theory beautiful. It is awe inspiring. It brings joy to those who see it and understand it.

That is the same way that I think and feel about the theological and intellectual foundations of Catholicism. Some of the greatest minds of all time have pondered the deepest and most complex questions of reality, many of which I have at least touched on earlier in this book. None of those great minds, and certainly not I, understand fully what reality is and what we propose as truth. But I think we are on the right track, because the theory…the theology…related to God, human beings, and the cosmos as a whole are addressed most completely and beautifully in Catholic thought. And it fills me with joy.

I love the Incarnational teachings of the Catholic Church. What that means is that material reality and human beings in particular, are shot through with the spiritual and the divine. God became a human being. Though God is something we struggle to comprehend, God, in the person of Jesus Christ, became one of us. Because of this, all of the material world, including ourselves, is raised up to a new level of being. That new level of being does not preclude or diminish our physicality or our humanity. Rather, it raises it to a new height of wonderfulness and completeness. And in the end, though we will die and our physicality will turn to dust, the Incarnational teachings of the Catholic Church say that we will rise again. That we will once again be a unique combination of body and spirit, because the body is good and so is the spirit.

Another aspect of the Catholic Church that I particularly like is the sacramental system that it uses. The Sacraments are another aspect of the Incarnational aspect of reality. The sacraments are visible and physical signs of interactions between us and God that encompass some of the more important aspects and milestones of our life from birth/Baptism to death/The Last Rites. In between are the sacraments of coming of age/Confirmation and marriage and family/Matrimony. For a few, there is the sacrament of Holy Orders, for those who will be priests. And, on an on-going basis, because we need them regularly, there are sacraments of the family meal/Holy Eucharist and forgiveness/Reconciliation. Within the teaching and practice of the Catholic Church, these sacraments raise our level of being and sustain us in our efforts to be who and what we can be and should be as human beings. They make the ordinary things in life holy and give us the wisdom, strength, and courage we need as we undertake the big decisions and events in our lives, as well as our daily struggles to survive and be good persons and happy persons.

I like a lot of the Scriptures and some I dislike. Some of the Scriptures seem to be caught in some horrible time warp of an agricultural/pastoral society and which reflect the patriarchal and monarchial societal structures of the times in which they were written. But some parts of Scripture are simply overwhelmingly, dead-on/insightful and beautifully poetic when speaking to our deepest hopes and desires as human beings. And sometimes the Scriptures are uncannily accurate and knowledgeable about human nature, our strengths and our weaknesses, and the practical ways in which our behaviors can help us be and do what we can and should do to be fully human and in harmony with ourselves and all of the realities around us.

Finally, I like the Catholic Church because it is the only organization I know of that has at the core of its beliefs and practice a "preferential option for the poor." I know that the Catholic Church has not always lived up to that concept and does not do so to the level I desire now. But that message and commitment is at the core of the Church's sociological and economic teaching. Different religions hold up different ideals for both individuals and societies to strive for. The bottom line in Scripture and the Catholic Church of how we will be judged as human beings on how we lived our lives is how we care for the poor, the sick, the homeless, the naked, the prisoner, etc. Seeking social and economic justice is at the core of who I am as an individual and it is at the core of what the Catholic Church stands for as an organization in time.

I will probably die a Catholic. I don't agree with some of their teachings. I think they are run by an insular group of old men who have limited understanding of the lives that people live and consequently, they propose doctrines and impose rules and regulations that are out of touch with reality. I have felt less and less welcome in the Catholic Church. I think that if they really knew what I thought about many things they teach that they would throw me out of the Church.

But that is okay. The Catholic Church often forgets that sinners are welcome. If I am a sinner in some ways because I don't agree with the Church, then so be it. The Church may not forgive me, but I think and believe God will.

In the meantime, I can participate in the sacramental and liturgical life of the Church, encountering and being in awe of God as best I can and living out the preferential option for the poor as best I can. Whether they want me or not, they've got me. I always thought of it a little like members of a family. None of us is perfect, but, as someone once said, a family are the ones that have to take you in when no one else will.

My theological beliefs and understandings and my religious life bring me great joy, peace and happiness. It doesn't diminish the sometimes harsh realities of life. As far as I am concerned, it does not put limits on my life experiences. To the contrary, it adds a dimension to my life that goes beyond the mere material world that I easily and readily encounter every day. I don't dismiss or devalue the realities of the everyday, material world. I enjoy them and I struggle with them like everyone else. But my religious beliefs and practices add a broader and deeper element to the spiritual realities within me, within others, and with the Spirit of God and my relationships with all of reality.

CHAPTER TWENTY

Praying For Wisdom, Strength, and Courage

Like most people, I always had a problem with not having prayers answered. We have all heard the quote, "Ask and it shall be given to you, seek and you will find, knock and it shall be opened to you." So, why doesn't someone get cured of cancer when I ask God to do so? Why isn't there peace in the Middle East when I ask God to accomplish that? Most importantly, why can't the Chicago Cubs win a World Series, or even get to one, when so many fervently pray for that to happen?

When I pray, I don't expect cures for my ailments, winning a game, good fortune for my family, etc. I don't think God intervenes in those matters very often or at all. Instead, I pray for wisdom, strength and courage. Those are qualities of the Spirit/spirit which the second half of the quote above makes reference to: "I will ask God to send you the Holy Spirit who will guide you."

My first request is to ask for wisdom.

Wisdom is a very broad term in my way of thinking.

Wisdom is a combination of knowledge and love (head and heart) that leads to practical action.

I pray for knowledge as an aspect of wisdom to help me understand as much as I can about a situation; to correctly identify the problem and core issue; to bring as broad an array of knowledge as I can and is relevant to the situation, taking into account a wide range of disciplines including, but not limited to: science, history, sociology, psychology, philosophy, economics, business, theology, etc.

I think that the more I know in as broad a range of relevant topics, the better decisions I can make.

I pray for and include love in my definition of wisdom because it adds a very important element to knowledge. I think that we know with both our head and our heart. Love is part of wisdom because it puts knowledge in perspective. Love speaks to the relational nature of people and things. Love is a choice; an act of will to choose the true, the good, and the beautiful. Love helps me choose what is good for me and for others (they are usually not mutually exclusive goals).

Through knowledge, we know as best we can <u>what is</u>.

Through love, we can apply that knowledge and make decisions about <u>what should be</u>.

Wisdom is the combination of mind and heart which helps us choose what is right…what is good…what promotes life and love.

In addition to wisdom and finding a course of action which is best to pursue, I pray for strength and courage to actually do it.

Though strength and courage are similar in many ways, they mean two different things to me when I pray.

Strength is the capability to act:

-To start something.

-To see it through.

-To not give up prematurely just because it gets tough.

I pray for strength to go from a state of inertia to a course of action. Wisdom without strength doesn't get the job done.

Courage is related to strength because it often takes courage to do what wisdom may lead us to do. The wise decision may require a new course of action that others may consider foolish, or a waste of time, or won't be successful. Wisdom sometimes leads us to a course of action which is not generally accepted by society. A wise course of action might actually cause people to want to harm us in some way. Sometimes it takes courage, because we may end up standing alone in our understanding of a situation and what we decide we should do about it. Sometimes it means risking failure. So I pray for courage.

I also pray for wisdom, strength, and courage to protect me from stubbornness and bullheadness, and sticking with a course of action until it hurts me or someone else. Wisdom knows when to stop a course of action if the circumstances change or we learn new things that should lead us to choose differently.

Our strengths are also often our weaknesses. Wisdom helps us see when our strength is killing us. It tells us when to change and helps us decide what to change and how to change.

So when I pray for wisdom, strength, and courage, I pray for help to see what truth, beauty, goodness, and love requires of me in a situation and then helps me to act on it.

The reason I pray for wisdom, strength, and courage is that I am pretty confident my prayer will be heard. I think and believe that God always grants wisdom to carry out God's work in our world. It is a Spirit to spirit, relational thing. It is like asking a good friend for advice and support. A good friend always will give it to us because they love us. If a good friend will give us her or his advice, love and support, how much more so will God give us wisdom when we ask for it? God grants us wisdom so our hearts and minds are led to be open to reality and to respond in a knowledgeable and loving way...a wise way...a way that promotes as much of a heaven on earth here and now that we are capable of doing.

And when I pray for others, I basically pray for the same things for them. Life can be challenging and hard as well as wonderfully enjoyable. When times are hard, whether due to our own actions, natural disasters, the actions of others, etc., I think the best we can do for ourselves and others is to move forward in our lives wisely, with courage and strength, and with dignity…making and carrying out decisions and actions that are worthy of the best that each of us is capable of doing.

But even then, I do not expect total success or some type of visible sign of God's intervention in response to my prayer. First of all, I don't know what total success in a particular situation might be. Sometimes it may take years to see the results of a decision and action. Also, I know for myself that, even with the guidance of God's Spirit, I still may not act appropriately. My tendencies to take action too quickly, or my anger, or my impatience, or my fear of the unknown may hinder the work of God's grace within me.

But at that point, I am at peace knowing that I have the help of God's Spirit to deal with whatever difficulties come my way. That doesn't mean that I sit back and wait for God to solve my problems. What it means is that I will do everything I can to solve the problem or face the challenges that confront me or others for whom I pray. But I know that in addition to bringing the best I have to the situation, God will help me understand and act as wisely as I or the people I pray for can do within our human limitations and circumstances.

CHAPTER TWENTY-ONE

Work

Most of us spend at least half of our waking hours every week working. We also spend at least a third of the hours in our lifetime working.

So, work is certainly one of the realities that almost all of us have to think about seriously and interact with as positively as we can.

The old adage is that we should find work that is our passion, and then it won't seem like work. It will be a joy to do our jobs every day.

Another old adage is that work is hard, and that's why they call it work.

Like most old adages, there are elements of truth in both of them.

I have found work to be both a joy at times and hard at other times, often while doing the same job; sometimes within the same hour or the same day.

Almost all of us have to do some type of work in order to support ourselves, and where applicable, other members of our family. When we start looking at the practicalities of how we will do that, I think we try to find some type of work we would enjoy, something that would allow us to use and develop our talents and skills, and something that would also help us meet our deepest motivations and goals. That's a lot to ask for in any aspect of our lives, let alone a job.

Having the freedom and opportunities to pursue a career that fits us is a fairly recent historical and economic event for most people who have worked through the whole history of time. Even today, there are many people who do not have many work options. But for those of us who have been fortunate enough to have been born into a country with an advanced economy, to have had a good education, and to have had job choices and opportunities, choosing a job or career is an important, and sometimes daunting, decision.

I think there are five things that are very important to think about when making decisions and choices regarding work and career:

- Enjoy the work.
- Be an opportunity to develop our talents and skills.
- Contribute to the co-creation of an evolving world.
- Balance our work life with the rest of our life.
- Be prepared to change to meet external economic circumstances and internal personal needs and desires.

First, enjoy the work. I think we are all good at some things. Doing work that is in harmony with who we are as an individual is very important. When we start thinking about a career and the work we will do, most of us don't know what type of work might be in harmony with who we are and what fits our inclinations and skills. We all probably know a few people who knew what they wanted to do from an early age. I think they are a rarity. Often those who know what they want to be when the grow up have had some experience at an early age that helped them define who they are and what type of work might fit with that. Often they have a role model that inspires them to do so.

One of the issues in determining what work we want to do when we grow up is that we often have no real idea of what it means to do certain work for a living and for a long period of time. It used to be that there was concreteness to the work that most of us could understand and relate to. Up until the last hundred years, most jobs for most people were things that young people experienced every day in their lives. They saw adults performing the work. Often, the young people might perform some of the work themselves (e.g., farming, carpentry, masonry, printing, and other trades).

But most of us don't really know what we want to be when we grow up. We are told to pursue the professions that are deemed to be signs of success because of the prestige and money associated with them (e.g., doctors, lawyers, engineers, CEO's in business, etc.). Or we are told to pursue entertainment or athletic careers which will bring us celebrity and money. Or we are told to choose a career which makes a contribution to a better world by being teachers, or social workers or counselors of one type or another, or nurses, or firefighters, or police officers or any of the helping professions.

All of these options and choices are reasonable ones. Some are more likely to be achieved than others (the percentage of athletes who make it to the pros is very, very small compared to those who would like to make it; the same with entertainers). Being a doctor or lawyer or a success in business is more achievable depending on our own skills, talents, capacity for hard work, and a certain amount of good luck.

One reason many of us try several different jobs as we go through school and we start our careers is that we really have to experience how a particular job and the related duties and responsibilities fit with our skills, talents, and interests. Being a "people person" in a people-related job is good if that is what fits you. Being a numbers person in a people-related job is a recipe for job dissatisfaction and unhappiness. We all have to understand what it is about ourselves that really is us and what brings us satisfaction and a sense of accomplishment. The next thing to do is then find a job which fits that.

Second, be an opportunity to develop our talents and skills. Once we find an area of work which fits us, it is important to find a job that also allows us to develop our talents and skills. Except for a few geniuses over the centuries (think Mozart, Einstein, and a few others), most of us don't hit our peak in our teens or early 20's. If we are going to enjoy our work, we also need the opportunity to grow and develop ourselves as human beings.

Sometimes we can do that at and through our work. Since we all spend so much of our life at work, I think it is ideal to find work that allows us to grow and develop. But I know that is not always the case for many people. So sometimes we can grow and develop through other parts of our lives (I have known some people who are tied into jobs that are not particularly satisfying, but they find other avenues to develop their skills and abilities through participation in other organizations or activities that meet their needs and desires for personal growth and development).

The fact that we want to grow and develop is at the core of who we are as human beings and we carry over that desire into our work life. One of our basic reasons for being is to flourish as a human being as discussed earlier. In a diverse and developed economy that we enjoy, most of us can take care of our basic needs of food, shelter, and clothing. Most of us live in a reasonably safe environment. So, developing ourselves as human beings and meeting our self-actualization needs is very important to all of us. And that self-actualization is not just an increase in our skill levels, in what we know, in what we can do and in what we *have*. Self-actualization makes us more of a human being. It makes us more fully what we *are* as a human being.

Work can give us a chance to grow and flourish as a human being, but usually not every hour of every day. Work can be a real pain sometimes. But over the long haul, we want our work to provide us the opportunity for such growth and development...the opportunity to flourish as a human being.

That sense of accomplishment and flourishing as a human being related to work is one reason why unemployment is so devastating to so many people. In our society, we are often judged by what we do and how successful we are. At the most fundamental level of human motivation is our need to provide the basics of food, clothing and shelter for ourselves and our family. If we do not have the opportunity to do that, it puts a great strain on ourselves as individuals and on those other people in our lives with whom we have close relationships. Unemployment causes a great deal of personal and family anguish. Unemployment is much more than an economics statistic. Those who are unemployed through no fault of their own are deeply and sorely touched by their circumstances. It is very difficult to flourish when a person cannot meet their basic survival needs through work.

One other aspect of work is the idea that "We become what we do." What I mean by that is that work requires us to adopt the value system of our employer or of the type of work that we do, no matter who is the employer. We are expected to do work in accordance with that value system. That can be good or bad. It can be good if the value system of our work environment is in agreement with what we think is important in our own total life value system. It can be detrimental to who we are and who we become if the value system of our work environment is in conflict with or over emphasizes one aspect of who we are as human beings to the detriment of who we are as total and complete human beings.

An example from the good side of value systems associated with work and organizations are the values associated with most professions. Practitioners are expected to be focused above all on maintaining high standards of work that serve the needs of others. Doctors, lawyers, nurses, police officers, firefighters, teachers, etc. are all expected to put the needs of their profession and the people they serve above their own personal needs. We know that does not always happen. But it is the ideal. The behaviors desired and required of those involved in a variety of types of professional and service-oriented work are compatible with what it means to be a good human being.

An extreme example from the bad side of value systems associated with work and organizations are some of the business practices that became almost a religious and moral system unto itself. "Greed is good," is a phrase that gained in credibility in the 1980's and 1990's. The basic justification for that value system was that it is a good thing for people to be greedy because it creates wealth for all. The other side of that value system is that if someone tries to do something from a non-economic, non-self-interest set of motivations, then that is considered to be a waste of resources and ultimately is irresponsible. "Greed is good" reached its disastrous conclusion in the Enron scandal and all of the other business scandals that surfaced in the recent past. The corruption fostered by the "Greed is good" value system led to the implosion of the Arthur Anderson auditing company. They betrayed the values of their profession in order to make money. Many people in the companies involved, and in the general public who owned stock in these companies, suffered a great deal from this work-related value system.

I think people who are in decision-making capacities in business have to be particularly careful of not adopting a set of values that over emphasizes making money. Making money is a good thing. It is the reason that any company goes into business. All of us need a strong economic system in which to live and flourish as individuals and as part of a community. But what has crept into the workplace on a much broader scale over the last 25 years is that making a profit is not enough. Companies and the people who own them think and feel that they have to maximize their profits. I think that value system is very detrimental to the overall happiness and flourishing of individuals who run those companies or work in those companies. Everything cannot and should not be reduced to an economic calculation. As human beings, we are more than that. When it comes to being truly happy, we short change ourselves and we short change others when the overriding value in our lives is maximizing company profits and/or our own material well-being. That is why I think it is a particularly difficult role to be in a leadership position in a private business today. I think it is difficult to not let the values that shape our decisions everyday in the business world spill over and unduly shape and influence our decisions in the rest of our lives. Making business decisions that maximize profits to the exclusion and detriment of other values that are important to the flourishing of individuals and groups can become part of our personal value system as a human being and cause us to lose sight of what is really important to us, and what will really make us and others happy and flourishing as human beings.

Third, contribute to the Co-Creation of an Evolving World. I think most of us, particularly when we are young and contemplating a career, at least had some desire to make a contribution to a better world. I think there are many ways to contribute to a better world.

That term means different things to different people. We usually associate that idea with being involved with one of the helping professions such as a doctor, nurse, or teacher. To some it means inventing a new product or discovering a cure for cancer. To some it is a call to public service or a religious life. To others it means creating a work of art which people find beautiful. And to yet others, the desire to entertain people is a motivator. The list is endless and I will not try to capture every type of work imaginable. I think the hard thing is finding a career which will blend the dual goals of making an adequate living and contributing to a better world.

Since how each of us does that is so unique to what our deepest motivations are, I would like to use, as an illustration, my own experience of meshing together my deepest motivations with making a living.

Making the world a better place was my primary motivator from as early on as I can remember. Making the world a better place meant giving people opportunities to grow and succeed; rewarding people for their hard work; treating people fairly; and creating and sustaining organizations and groups which contributed to that. Making the world a better place was something I internalized as a place to put my skills and talents to work, and hopefully, to make a living at. It was, from one perspective, a very secular approach to changing things for the better. And that was fine. But considering my religious background and training, it was also a calling or vocation that echoed one of the most important directives that I remember from the Gospels: "Feed the poor, clothe the naked, take care of the sick, visit the imprisoned, etc." So, I thought I had a pretty clear direction of what I would do when I grew up. I wasn't aware of what the specific job might be, but I was sure that it would be something that would try to make the world a better place.

As I learned more about a broad range of things, I began to see my work with an additional dimension. I always saw making the world a better place as a good thing to do for the people in the world now. But as I learned more about evolution and science in general, I began to see another dimension to my work that was even more exciting and challenging.

As I mentioned in different places in several earlier chapters, I think the world is evolving and can evolve to a better entity. It is, in a sense, that the world is continuing to be created. And we, as intelligent, self-aware, and choosing human beings, can co-create the future with others and with God. I truly believe that we are all called to bring the world closer to the best that it can be, not only in terms of human beings, but the entire physical world that we all interact with.

I think and believe that it can be done. I don't think any of us has the power or ability to change everything, but I do think all of us are able to change some things for the better. I think we can do it from both organizational and individual perspectives and impacts.

Trying to make the world a better place has been, and still is, work that I truly enjoy. It fits me. It has allowed me many opportunities to use my skills and abilities, and to also grow them. I have had a lot of satisfaction in my work. The philosophical and religious motivations I bring to my work, even when it is difficult, have helped me enjoy my work more than I would have done so without those motivations.

One of the things related to making and co-creating a better world is that it has always led me to do the best job I can on any job I have taken or assignment I have been given. Every time I approach a task, I do it with the understanding that if I do it to the best of my ability, I bring some measure of truth, beauty, and/or goodness into the world. Maybe it is wishful thinking. But based on all of the discussions in earlier chapters and how I see each of us living and flourishing as human beings, engaged with the realities in us and around us, I derive a great deal of peace and satisfaction in doing my work, whatever it is. How could I do less than my best when if I do my best, I further the co-creation of the kind of world we all would like it to be for ourselves and for others including our children and grand children? And, at the same time, I am advancing the ultimate reality of the loving union of all of reality with each other and with God. Every individual or group I meet and interact with and every project I undertake is an opportunity to encounter reality and make it better.

Almost any line of work any of us chooses to do can be a contribution to a better world as long as it is done well, that is, to the highest standards of the type of work we choose or are able to perform.

Fourth, balance our work life with the rest of our life. This is a very difficult thing to do. And, it is something that must be addressed over and over throughout our work life. We may find a balance between our work life and the other parts of our life at one particular time, but we may change jobs or the job requirements of our current job may change. Our life circumstances outside of work also change. With all of these changes, we regularly need to find a new balance between work and the rest of our life.

I don't know what the balance is for any particular person. Again, I would like to use myself to illustrate some of these points. Work is important to me. I am capable of doing a great deal of work. I am focused when I work. I usually get more work done than most people I have worked with over the years. I do high-quality work. Because of all of those things, I have been successful in most things that I have undertaken from a work standpoint. But I have always been careful to maintain a reasonable balance between my work and the rest of my life, particularly my relationships with my immediate family.

Over the years, I have been in very demanding work positions. I have not enjoyed a forty-hour work week for many weeks of my adult life. Usually, I have worked 50 to 60 hours a week and often more. Also, my work has often involved travel around the country. And, even though travel to and from clients is usually not considered direct work, it takes time away from other parts of your life.

Two things have always been touchstones for me for finding a reasonable balance between work and the rest of my life. One touchstone has to do with defining priorities in my life and then making work and non-work decisions based on those priorities. The second touchstone is how my relationships with my immediate family are faring. This second touchstone is really a subset of the first, because the well being of my family has always been one of my highest priorities. And I consider it an important touchstone, because it was something I could monitor on a regular basis. Setting priorities can be a somewhat sterile intellectual exercise. But paying attention to and judging the quality of my relationships with my spouse and children is a real life test of whether or not the balance between work and the rest of my life is where it should be.

There is often no end to the demands that work can make on us. Do a good job and the expectation levels of our employers often rise and require us to do more and to do better. Also, work can often be less demanding of our skills and abilities than developing and maintaining good family relationships. I think it is easier for many people, particularly men, to work than to be attentive to family relationships.

Finally, we often have to make conscious decisions to devote time to our family relationships. Again, work will usually demand more and more of our time, if we let it. Good relationships with our spouses and children don't just happen. They must be consciously worked at and developed. We spend most of our waking hours working. So that aspect of our lives will always demand our time and attention. And, we are often taught and trained on how to do well at our work.

Seldom are we formally taught and trained on how to develop and improve our family relationships. Most of what we have learned about family relationships has come from our experiences growing up in a family. For some people who had good examples of how a family can be a positive and supportive network of relationships, translating that experience into our own lives is easier. But many have not had good examples of positive family relationships on which to build their family life. We often consider it something that should take care of itself. We consider it something that will just happen as long as we bring home a paycheck and not be a mean person in our family relationships. Family relationships need nurturing, care, and attention if they are to succeed, grow, and develop.

As far as priorities are concerned, that has always been a particular challenge for me. I am interested in all kinds of topics, issues, and activities. It is nice to have a lot of interests, but it means that I have to regularly turn down things to do. I sometimes wish I had several lifetimes to live so that I could try and do the many things that interest me. But being a mere mortal like everyone else (unless the reincarnation folks are correct), I have had to limit what I would and could do.

Everything takes time, and there are limited hours available to all of us. Where I put my time is based on my priorities. As I have stated earlier, my priorities are as follows:

1. Support my family.
2. Have good relationships with my wife and children.
3. Have a job or jobs that fulfill my first priority, but also give me the opportunity to make a difference in the world.
4. Be in relationship to God.
5. Have good relationships with my larger family.
6. Take care of my health so I can accomplish the above items and be around for the long run.

Giving time and effort to those priorities and doing them as well as I can is pretty much a full time job. Everything else that does not fit into that is really a very low priority. As much as I enjoy sports (as both a participant and fan) and the full-range of arts (plays, opera, the symphony, art galleries, etc.), I have had to minimize my engagement with those elements in my life. I have had to minimize my time for friendships with other people and mostly confine them to work situations. Part of that limitation on friendships is because I come from a large family (nine brothers and sisters, numerous cousins, nephews and nieces). I have many relationships within my broader family that I consider friendships. I have had to consciously decide not to have more friendships with non-family members.

One last thought about balancing work and the rest of our lives that I think is important: remember the words, "Less money and more fun!" We all need to support ourselves and our families. But making more money by spending more and more time on work-related activities has a diminishing effect on our lives overall. "All work and no play makes Jack a dull boy (or Jill, a dull girl)!" is another old adage that still has some truth in it. There is really more wonderfulness to life than can be experienced through work. Certainly work can be a very fulfilling and happiness producing activity as discussed earlier. But it is only one aspect of our life as full human beings. Work can help us flourish as human beings, but it also can limit our lives from experiencing the other wonderful and beautiful things in life. Again, there are only so many hours in the day and we have only so much energy to devote to life's activities: so, to limit our range of life's experiences to work-related activities is detrimental to our happiness and flourishing as human beings as described earlier.

Fifth, be prepared to change to meet external economic circumstances and internal personal needs and desires. The era of a lifetime career with one company has been over for 20 years. Many jobs which were the base of the economy 30, 40, and 50 years ago have disappeared. They have either been eliminated as jobs or replaced by technology or, in America at least, they have been outsourced to other countries. On the other hand, many of the jobs today never existed 50 years ago. More than likely, the pace of change in jobs and types of work will continue to accelerate in the future.

It has become a cliché to say that most people will have three or four different careers over their lifetime. But, like most clichés, it has a lot of truth in it. Besides changes in the external workplace, there are also a number of factors affecting internal, personal needs and desires.

First of all, people are living longer. They are able to work to an older age. Years ago, when most of the jobs required hard and repetitive manual labor, peoples' bodies broke down under the physical strain, wear, and tear. Today, most work is not as physically taxing. Consequently, people can work longer if they need and/or want to.

Second, many people need to work longer these days. The average life span has increased by approximately ten years since the 1940's when I was born. In those days, living to 65 meant you were old, and you were considered to probably have one foot in the grave.

If you made it into your early 70's, you were one of the lucky ones. The good news these days is that, on average, we are living longer. The bad news is that it takes significantly more money to support ourselves after we "retire."

Third, there is a growing desire on the part of individuals to have variety in their work. It was one thing to do a job for twenty-five or thirty years, and then retire. It is another thing to have a work career spanning forty or fifty years. Some careers lend themselves to growth and change that someone might find interesting for such a long span of time. But most do not. Also, I have found for myself that there are so many different things that I find interesting and could do, that it is hard to limit my areas of work. I think we all have to limit our career choices in order to succeed in our work. We all have to have some marketable skill set and body of knowledge to sell in a more segmented economy that generally requires and rewards specialization.

Fourth, and finally, many people simply cannot stop working. So much of their life has been built around their work that stopping their work is like a death sentence. Many people have derived their reason for being and their sense of self-worth from their work. Certainly, work is an important element in our sense of ourselves. But work that is done to the detriment of the rest of our lives is not good for us or those with whom we have close relationships.

I think all of us have to prepare ourselves to work a longer time than previous generations. I think we need to be lifelong learners, including understanding and using technology which will continue to rapidly evolve in the workplace and in our lives in general. We need to stay healthy and capable of working. And, I think we need to keep alive our sense of wonder and awe at the world in which we encounter in different ways everyday so that our enthusiasm for being part of the re-creation of the world does not falter.

CHAPTER TWENTY-TWO

What is Marriage?

Most of us want to love and be loved.

That desire and need is at the core of who we are as human beings.

There are many ways to love and be loved, but for most of us that means getting married. Marriage isn't essential to loving and being loved, but it is the most common path human beings take to try and achieve that goal.

What is marriage?

I think, in its best sense, it is an interpersonal relationship which embodies a commitment that two people make to each other to love the other person and to share their total being, including their bodies and their life. Usually, it is a commitment that people make and hope will last for a lifetime.

In addition to the interpersonal relationship, but not always, marriage is also a preferred arrangement and associated commitment to bring children into the world and to raise them together, as a couple. Having children is not essential to marriage, but until fairly recently due to more effective birth control methods, it has been an almost universal result of marriage.

Marriage is also a social, economic, and legal construct. Society needs some types of structures so that it can function effectively. This is particularly true as societies grow and become more complex.

Marriage is a social construct for two main reasons. First, for most of history, women and wives were considered as property of the

males and husbands. Some structure was needed to define and protect the male's right to his spouse/child bearer/chattel, etc. Second,
since having children has been a pretty universal result of marriage,
some structures needed to be in place to protect and foster the growth
and development of children. It takes a long time for a human being
to move from birth to independence. Parents have always had individual responsibilities regarding raising a child. Also, the clan, tribe,
or village has had varying degrees of responsibility for seeing that
their group replenished itself with their young. Continuing as a tribe
or nation was not guaranteed when a lot of the laws related to marriage and family were instituted to foster the growth of the family,
and by extension, the tribe and the nation.

Marriage is an economic construct from two main perspectives.
First, some structure needs to be in place so that the economic
resources necessary to raise children can be ensured. Marriage was
less important in this regard when society was smaller and less complex and/or when the idea of private property was not as strong as it
is today. Two adults pooling efforts and resources had a better chance
of survival for themselves and their children. Such is the case
whether both adults are working the fields in an agricultural society
or earning money in an industrialized society. Second, some structure needs to be in place so that property and other economic
resources could be shared between the marriage partners and passed
on from generation to generation. There needs to be some system
that identifies family relationships so that parentage is clear and
inheritance of resources can occur.

Marriage is also a legal construct. As societies grew and
became more complex, human activities of all kinds became the subject of a legal code and system of laws. Many of the laws affecting
marriage are related to the economic aspects of marriage and family.

Many of the laws were, and still are, also related to power and control of women by men.

Finally, marriage often has a religious element to it. A lot of the religious ideas regarding marriage and family were attempts to codify and regularize the social, economic, and legal structures spoken to above. Marriage rites and ceremonies were adopted to solemnize the bond between the marriage partners and to invoke the gods of fertility so that the family and society could survive and prosper. Religious practices over the centuries have recognized and sanctioned many types of marriage and family relationships.

Some of the earliest religious laws related to marriage and family were based on fostering the survival and growth of the society and the religion at a time when the number of people in the society mattered. Sexual practices which worked against building up the number of offspring were determined to be evil. Sexual activities which led to sexually transmitted diseases (multiple partners) or did not lead to procreation (homosexuality and masturbation) or muddied the waters of parentage (adultery) were banned religiously and often legally. Many of those same religious prohibitions exist today even though having multiple births to support the tribe or nation are not major concerns or goals of most societies and individuals. Religious laws have also embodied and sanctioned male dominance in marriage and family relationships, and by extension, the dominance by males in society in general.

From a positive sense, religions and theology have often proposed and fostered the idea that marriage and family are the basic human relationships which provide the framework and opportunities for human beings to learn about, practice, and grow in love, both human and Divine.

There is much more that can be said about marriage and family. Marriage and family are complex subjects and realities. Some elements have remained constant and some have changed significantly over the years. Today's concepts and structures evolved from the past individual and societal circumstances. It is likely that some of those concepts and structures will change in the future. But whatever the concepts and structures are or become, they need to address the interpersonal, societal, economic, legal, and religious elements that constitute marriage and families. So too, does our own approach to making decisions and living our lives in regards to marriage and family.

CHAPTER TWENTY-THREE

Why Get Married Today?

First of all, I don't think it is mandatory that people who want to have a loving relationship get married. I think marriage provides some legal and economic protections and rights to married people that they do not have if they are not married. But in and of itself, if the marriage is only about the relationship between the two adults, marriage in a secular world is not necessary.

The picture changes when children that result from the relationship are involved. Then the societal, economic, and legal structures that protect the interests of the child and often the less economically independent adult in the relationship, make marriage a more compelling argument, if not for the adults involved, then at least for the child or children. Again, I don't think it is absolutely essential that the parents of a child be married. But then, bringing a human life into the world moves the discussion from the somewhat limited scope of what is necessary and desirable from the adults' relationship standpoint to the broader scope of what is good for all of the members of the relationship, particularly the more dependent members which are always the children involved and, very often, the mother of the child or children.

But whether or not society, economics, the legal system or religious rules make sense to someone to get married, I think there are a number of good reasons for people to get married whether or not there are children involved.

The primary reason I think people who love each other and want to have a long-term relationship should get married is because it creates the best environment and circumstances for two people to flourish as human beings and be happy. Marriage provides the opportunity for each partner to become more of what a human being is and wants to be.

The aspects of the marriage environment and circumstances which contribute to mutual, personal development are several:

- Commitment
- Opportunities to Know and Understand Reality
- Opportunities to Grow in Love

Commitment is the decision to pursue something worthwhile. It can be a commitment to a person, a sport, a job, an artistic talent, etc. None of us can be and do everything. We need to make choices among many good things in order to focus our talents and energies on some aspects of reality. Commitment is often looked at as a limitation. And in some ways it is. But we are limited beings. In order to excel at anything, we need to limit our range of activities and focus our talents and energies on what we can succeed at. Since loving and being loved is so important to each of us as human beings, most of us have the best chance of succeeding and flourishing in that part of our lives if we make a commitment to be in a loving relationship with another person.

That commitment then gives us the opportunities to grow in knowledge and understanding of one of the most important aspects of reality: what it means to be a human being capable of knowing and loving. That knowledge will come about if we are committed to making the relationship last, almost in spite of everything (I say almost in spite of everything, because some relationships may never grow and develop or may even become abusive and detrimental to one or both parties to the relationship. In such cases, the relationship should end.).

In order to know the other person in the relationship, we have to first know ourselves as a unique person who is a material and spiritual entity worthy of respect and love. We then have to know the other person as the unique person that they are and who is also worthy of respect and of being known and loved. A committed interpersonal relationship is a continuous learning process regarding the most important entities in all of reality: who and what we are as unique human beings. Trying to know and understand the other person as who they truly are and not as we hope they are or think they are, is one of the most important learning processes that a human being can be engaged in. Knowing other things in life is important, too. But self-aware and self-reflective knowing are capacities and qualities that are unique to human beings. In order to be happy and flourish as human beings, we need to develop those capacities and expand our knowledge and understanding of ourselves and the other person with whom we have a committed relationship.

Learning what it means to be a human being and to be in relationship to another human being through being a part of a committed relationship then spreads out to other persons. That knowledge gives us the capacity to interact with other human beings in a more profound and deeper level. It allows us to first respect and then know others better than if we had not developed that knowledge about ourselves and about others.

It really works both ways. We can't gain true and deep knowledge of ourselves without being in close and regular interaction with other human beings. A committed relationship, such as the one formalized in marriage, helps us do that.

That commitment and the opportunities for profound understanding then give us the opportunities to love and be loved. It gives us the opportunities to grow in love in relationship to the person with whom we have a committed relationship, as well as other human beings with whom we have relationships. It gives us the opportunities to do things for another person that fulfills their needs. Not the needs we think they have, but the needs that they really have.

And, the deeper the knowledge and understanding of the uniqueness and wonderfulness of the other person, the more we want to be one with that person. That oneness is not only a oneness of mind and spirit (as it is in friendship, for example), but in marriage, it is also a oneness of body. The more we know and love another person, the more we want to be one with that person in every aspect of ourselves as human beings.

Desiring to be one with another person naturally leads to a sexual attraction; and that sexual attraction then leads to a sexual relationship between two people who know and love each other deeply. The sexual relationship which results from a deep mutual knowledge and love between two human beings is an end in itself and worthy of being pursued by human beings. And the sexual relationship is also an opportunity to know ourselves and the person with whom we are having the relationship in a more personal and deep way. The physical relationship feeds the spirit and vice-versa.

One of the paradoxes of being a human being is that we want to be ourselves as individuals while at the same time being one with others. The wonderful thing about having a deep and abiding love for another person is that we can have both. Through love, we become more of who we are and what we can be as a human being while at the same time becoming more one with the person with whom we are having the loving relationship.

Though all of us are sexually attracted to other human beings based on a number of superficial characteristics (and that is a good thing), one of the greatest sexual attractions, and an attraction that can deepen and last for a lifetime, is the relationship of the spirits between two people. Having a sexual relationship based primarily on the physical can be enjoyable for a while. But it will never last. The physical is usually the origin of the attraction, but as human beings, we want more than the physical. We want a human relationship which makes each of us more of what it means to be a human being as an individual and in relationship to another person.

CHAPTER TWENTY-FOUR

Why Do So Many Marriages Fail?

As I described marriage above, I think the makings of happiness are within such a relationship. But as we are all aware, happiness does not necessarily flow from having a spouse. In fact, for many people, marriage is a great source of unhappiness. The main reasons so many marriages fail are the following:

- People don't know what they are getting into.
- They don't pick their partner well.
- They don't know how to make a marriage successful.
- They don't change and grow.

People Don't Know What They Are Getting Into

People do not understand what marriage is because they don't understand who and what they are as human beings and what will truly make them happy. We all want to love and be loved. People understand that as a broad concept, but unless they understand love as a

- Relational connection between two people that is
- Mutually open to and accepting of the other person,
- Desires and acts for the well-being of the other person, and has, at its core,
- The desire to be one with that person.

136

the chances of the marriage lasting as a happy relationship are limited.

When most people get married, whether they are consciously aware of it or not, they have entered into and are experiencing love as described above. It is an exhilarating and happiness producing experience. Generally, both parties to a marriage are experiencing the joy and happiness which comes from loving and being loved at the core of who they are as human beings. Both people do connect at a deeper level of who each of them is in themselves and with each other. And, since the experience is so positive and happiness producing, people want to try and make it last forever. So they get married. And, they expect, or at least hope, that the excitement and happiness associated with the beginnings of a loving relationship will last forever.

Unfortunately, most people don't know what they have really encountered and experienced when they "fall in love." They know they are attracted to each other in many ways, including sexually. And, if they become sexually involved, the feelings of happiness usually are intensified and feed back into the close personal and spiritual bond that is beginning to develop between them. And, in many ways, all of that is good and fine; and it is the way most people begin a loving relationship which results in marriage.

The problem is that they really are not consciously aware of what they are experiencing that is making them so happy. Certainly the enjoyment related to the sexual relationship is consciously understood. But they do not know that what they are experiencing is just the beginning of a close, interpersonal, spirit to spirit, loving relationship as well. The beginning of a loving relationship is a great experience. But it is just that…a beginning. The relationship will not continue to exist, and hopefully, grow and flourish so that the happiness continues and deepens, unless both parties understand what they are involved in and make conscious choices and decisions to have that loving relationship grow and deepen.

They Don't Pick Their Partner Well

This is a toughie. Most people get married for the first time when they are relatively young. They don't know themselves that well yet. Usually, they know the person they are going to marry even less than they know themselves. They often don't have a very good idea of what it means to be married. And the examples of happily married couples are sometimes few and far between in some young peoples' lives.

So there are a lot of variables and unknowns when someone picks a spouse. That doesn't mean it can't be done well. And if it is going to have a chance of being a successful and happy, long-term marriage there are several key elements both parties should be thinking about:

1. Marry a good friend. Marry someone with whom you can and do have intimate conversations about who each of you is and what each of you hope for. And as good friends, be on the giving and receiving end of decisions and actions which each of you do for the other's happiness as the other defines her or his happiness.

2. Marry someone who has good values and with whom you share values regarding what is important to each of you in life.

3. Marry someone who treats you and others with respect. Don't marry a bully or a person who tries to force their will upon you and others, and treats others shabbily.

4. Marry someone who tries to understand who you are and not who they want you to be.

5. Be good friends before having sexual relations with the other person. Sex before marriage is pretty commonplace these days. But sex is such a powerful motivator and factor in our lives that the fun and pleasure of sex can obscure the joy and happiness that is coming from the budding close human relationship between the two people. It confuses the joy of loving and being loved with the joy of sex. Both are good things, but they should be thought about as two different elements in the mix of attractions between two people.

6. Wait approximately a year from the time you fall in love with someone until you decide to marry that person. Go through a year's cycle of life's ups and downs and see how both of you handle them.

There is a certain amount of luck in picking a marriage partner. When we are picking someone, we seldom know the other person in the depth that is necessary to guarantee a successful marriage. Some people fool us. Some talk a good game but don't deliver. Sometimes we are so desperate to love and be loved that we project our hopes and desires onto the other person rather than looking at who they really are. Like most of the difficult choices and matters in life, there are no guarantees. But we can all increase our odds of making better choices in all important areas of our lives if we know what we are aiming for and take reasonable steps to assess the pros and cons of a situation before making a decision. It is no different in picking a spouse.

They Don't Know How to Make a Marriage Successful.

How could anything as wonderful as falling in love disappear? Shouldn't it last forever, especially if both parties want it to last forever?

Unfortunately, like most things in life, wishing doesn't make it so.

Falling in love is somewhat serendipitous. More often than not, it just happens. As the old song goes,

> *You're walking along the street, or you're at a party,*
> *Or you're in a dim café, ordering wine,*
> *Then suddenly there she is,*
> *You want to be where she is,*
> *And this could be the start of something big!*

And though love often comes as a surprise, the reality is that it will not last unless it is consciously cultivated.

Most of us spend the majority of our waking hours working. If we want to succeed at our work, we learn what it takes to succeed. We spend many hours trying to do things better. We read about our work. We try to learn techniques which will help us accomplish more. We do not expect that the skills and talents with which we walk into a job will see us through until we retire.

Frankly, it is no different in succeeding in a marriage. But most of us are never told that and most of us have not seen that behavior modeled by other married people. We must give the relationship building and maintenance the time and effort it needs to succeed. Some time must be devoted each week to consciously and deliberately building and maintaining a mutually satisfying relationship.

In order for a marriage to happily succeed over the long run, both parties have to agree (ideally the agreement is explicitly committed to and not tacitly assumed) that making the marriage a success is a high priority to both of them and that they are willing to give time to each other to achieve that goal.

Learning and practicing good communications skills is one of the essential elements in building and maintaining a long-lasting relationship. Really listen to, talk with, and share your heart, mind and dreams with the other person. Being honest and open in those communications is essential and builds trust. No two people will ever agree on everything. Total agreement is not the goal of communication. Mutual understanding of each other is the goal. The deeper the mutual understanding and knowledge, the better chance there is of making successful decisions and taking actions which will be mutually beneficial. And as part of open and honest communication, actually value your differences. See them as a source of strength to complement each other. And refrain from saying mean or spiteful things to hurt the other person. If we are really close to another person, we know what will hurt them most deeply. To turn such knowledge, born of intimacy, into a mode of attack is one of the worst things people can do in a relationship. It eats away at trust and mutual respect. A person will start protecting themselves from attack by not sharing their minds and their bodies as openly and completely as they should. Mean and hurtful words turn sex into a duty or chore rather than one aspect of the total openness and acceptance of the other person which sex, at its best, signifies.

Another essential element is to do nice things for the other person several times a week for no specific reason other than that it makes the other person happy. It can be small things as well as larger things. But the opportunities to please the other person in small ways are easy to do and there are usually abundant opportunities. The key is paying attention to what pleases the other person…what makes them happy, not what we think should make them happy. Making time to talk and listen to each other, and be genuinely interested in the other person, is a gift that costs nothing but can be given regularly. Every person is different. So what we do for the other person has to fit and please them. That takes some attention and it takes some time. Not an overwhelming amount of either. But enough to keep both people pleased with the care and attention they are getting from the other.

Keep romance alive. The best way to keep a long-term sexual relationship alive is to have the sex flow from and be the result of the mutual love as described above. Sex can be recreational and fun. But sex is not love. It is an expression of love between two people who want to be one with each other in spirit and body. Like every aspect of real love, sexual relations should be mutually engaged in and enjoyed. Pleasure should be given and received in the way the partner wants it and which is not hurtful to either partner. Like anything else worthwhile, a sexual relationship over a longer period of time has to be consciously pursued, learned about from each other, and be open to change as the circumstances of life change. Spontaneous sex is good and fun, and should be enjoyed. But the opportunities and desire for spontaneous sex become more problematical as the realities of life become more complex. Time limitations, children's needs, job demands, varying degrees of ill health…all kinds of things, make it difficult to have a positive, enjoyable, and regular sexual relationship. Finding times and opportunities to not only have physical sex but to engage in the communication and closeness that leads to sex don't just occur. They have to be mutually planned for and pursued.

Balance each of your needs, goals, dreams, and careers - you both can't have everything at the same time. Balance the sacrifices you make for each other. Too often women have been expected to subordinate themselves to the needs and goals of their husbands and children. That is generally not a healthy situation for a long-term, successful, and happy relationship. That support role may fit some women, and if so, they should choose it. But it is not role that most women want any more than it is the role most men want.

And don't subordinate the roles of either of the marriage partners to economic considerations. Certainly every couple and every family have economic needs. But most of the economic expectations thrust upon people and which they incorporate into their lives are way oversold. Every child does not need their own bedroom. They don't need a car when they become 16. The family does not need an entertainment center with a huge TV and surround sound. Families don't have to go to Disney World to have a good family experience. Adults and children want loving time and attention. If they have that...going for a walk or taking a bike ride together or playing catch or many other one-on-one or intimate family activities... that is all the fun that most children and adults want. It takes time to make the money to have the "fun" that we are sold. In many cases, it siphons off parents' time for each other and for their children to the detriment of the relationships between them. If it is a choice between money and time, take the time, particularly with your spouse and children.

They don't change and grow.

This topic should really fit under the previous topic, but it is so key to having a successful marriage that it should be addressed separately.

We live in a world of constant change. Whether it is technology, popular culture, our jobs, the general economy, our health, and simply our aging, we are always experiencing change. In order to have a long-term, successful and loving relationship and marriage, both parties have to be open to change. We have to be open to how we ourselves change as well as how the other person changes. We have to be open to the changing circumstances within which we live as individuals and as a couple. And being confronted by change, we must change our behaviors regarding ourselves and how we relate to the other person.

This means we must grow our capacities as human beings to understand as best we can the true realities outside of ourselves and to respond to those realities in an authentic and genuine human way. We are not the same person at 25 that we were when we were 15. And we will not be the same person at 50 that we are at 25. Certainly there will be continuities in who and what we are as individuals whether we are 15, 25 or 50. But to live a successful and enjoyable life, a life in which we flourish as a human being, we need to change and adapt to the changing realities inside and outside of ourselves. We must recognize that the person with whom we are having a loving relationship will also change over the years. Again, there will be continuities regarding who that person is. But that person will change just as we will change. Both parties in a long-term loving relationship must understand that this occurs and that it takes an ongoing conversation and sharing of who each of us is as unique human beings for the long-term relationship to be happy.

Don't do stupid things.

No matter how much we are in a loving relationship with another person, it does not mean that we are not attracted to other people or that other people might not find us attractive. Going to a party or a bar with co-workers or friends without your spouse is asking for trouble. Having a social evening of drinks and dinner with a person of the opposite sex after work is dumb. Some people think they can handle and incorporate extra-marital affairs in their life without messing up their relationship with their spouse. They are fooling themselves. Except for the most duplicitous personalities, who most people would not want to be married to anyway, most people can't carry off affairs without it eventually negatively impacting their marriage. There are the extreme cases such as occurs in the cautionary movie "Fatal Attraction." But those types of things don't happen too often. What does happen is that people begin affairs as flings and recreational breaks. But having an extramarital affair is a little like starting a war. People think they know how to handle it and control it; but, like war, an affair often takes on a life of its own. War is difficult to control because it unleashes very deep emotions in all of the parties involved. Sexual relations also unleash very powerful emotions in both parties. Unless a person is willing to risk losing their loving relationship, he or she should not put herself in a position where having an affair becomes more likely or easier to accomplish. And that risk becomes greater when children may be the result of the original loving relationship and would be negatively affected by a split between the parents of the children.

When things don't work out as hoped for

Fortunately for most of us, we live long lives. Most laws and ideals related to monogamy were developed in times when people's life spans were relatively short. Living with someone for 10 or 15 years before the woman died in childbirth or the man was killed in a war or while hunting is pretty much a thing of the past. "Till death do us part" did not have the same meaning in people's lives when the average life span was around 40 years. Being married for the long run, though often held up as the ideal, was seldom tested in reality. So, I do not find it unreasonable that if a marriage never develops into the type of loving friendship which I have described previously, then the couple should mutually end it and seek another, hopefully more happiness producing, relationship.

I do not think that people have to stay married forever, but dissolving the marriage should not be done lightly. Neither party to a marriage is perfect. Both parties have to accept and live with each other's shortcomings, as long as the shortcomings are not abusive of the other party. Also, some marriages are just bad matches. Poor choices in a partner can sometimes be overcome, but not always. Sometimes trust and openness that is lost can be regained, but not always. If the marriage is not providing the happiness that both parties in the relationship want, then both parties should discuss the matter and proceed to dissolve the relationship. If one party is abusive to the other person, then the abused party should take steps to get out of the relationship.

Again, as the old song goes, "Breaking Up is Hard To Do." But sometimes it must be done. The term broken heart is appropriate when a relationship ends. A heart does break, because the end of a loving relationship means that we are not loved by someone with whom we probably had the start of a mutually loving relationship which did not grow and flourish. There is the disappointment of not seeing something continue that we very much wanted to continue, because whether or not we can articulate the reason behind the hurt caused by a breakup, we feel it. We also feel the pain of a breakup because we do want to love and be loved at the very core of who we are as human beings. And when a real or potential, mutually loving relationship ends, we do feel the pain of loss, disappointment, and a void in what we want to be and could be as human beings.

In summary, I think most of us as human beings want to have a long, loving and happiness-producing marriage. I think the opportunity to do so is there for most people. But we need to look at it and approach it as outlined above. Then it is a great joy. The love of both persons for each other grows and deepens. Both can become more of what it means to be a human being. Very few things in life are as happiness producing as being in a mutually loving relationship. It is worth the effort. That is why most of us instinctively pursue it, even though we may not have found that mutually loving relationship the first time around.

CHAPTER TWENTY-FIVE

Raising Children

Raising children well, like anything else, requires that we know what we are aiming for. If we do not have a clear idea of what we aiming for in raising children, the chances of doing it successfully are diminished. And like most other important things in life, we are given very little formal teaching and training in the matter. Most people raise their children as some offshoot of how they were raised, positively and negatively.

So, what are we aiming for when we raise children? I would suggest the following:

Developing a human person who flourishes as
-a unique combination of body and spirit,
-who exists in relationship to other things and people, and
-who has the capacity of:

- *Learning and knowing.*
- *Self-awareness, subjective knowledge, self-consciousness.*
- *Imagination and creativity.*
- *Evaluating and choosing.*
- *Loving and being loved.*

That is a tall order. It is a long-term goal. And, it must be achieved within a real world with many variables regarding each child, ourselves as parents, and outside influences which we cannot frequently fully understand, predict, or control. None of us will succeed 100% in achieving the goal. But we can give our children a good start to becoming flourishing human beings if we do the following:

- Love our children.
- Respect our children
- Give them the time they need.

Love Our Children

Love is a relational connection between two people which is mutually open to and accepting of the other person, desires and acts for the well-being of the other person, and, has at its core, the desire to be one with that person.

The loving relationship between parent and children has some different qualities to it than the loving relationship between two adults. At least for a number of years, children are not fully developed as human beings in the sense that their specifically human capacities of knowing and loving are in the earliest developmental stages. They are not always capable of knowing, loving, and acting in a way that is in their own best interests. So the role of the parents is to make certain decisions for the children which will allow them to grow and flourish.

Love takes different forms at different stages of children's lives. In the early years of child development, one of the most important things we can do for our children is to hold them and hug them, and have as much loving and affectionate physical contact with the child as possible. We never get those first few years back. It is extremely important for children to experience that physical affection, because it teaches them that they are loved and cared for. Children learn in their basic wiring what it means to be loved.

Children do not understand love as adults do. All that children can comprehend, in their deepest physical and developing emotional and psychological understanding and being, is what it feels like to be loved and cherished, and wanted for no other reason than because they exist and are therefore loved. That is the core of developing self-love and self-esteem in children. Later in life, doing things and accomplishing things can build children's self-love and self-esteem. But as babies and during the first few years of life, children should learn in their guts that they are loved simply because they exist. That is what we all want as adults and that is what all new children coming into the world want and need. Everything else is secondary. The clothes children wear, the schools they go to, and the talents they have certainly have some bearing on their well-being. But nothing is as important that we can give our children as the feeling and knowledge at the very core of who they are that they are loved, simply because they exist.

Another aspect of loving our children is to teach them to live healthily. That involves encouraging healthy physical activity and developing healthy eating habits. It is a great disservice to children to not lead and help them develop good health habits. Sugared cereals, snacks, pop, fruit drinks, etc., etc. abound on supermarket shelves. Children do not need them no matter how many television commercials tell them and us what fun it is to eat such aptly named junk food. Video games are fine in limited doses, but there are so many other stimulating mental and physical activities that children will enjoy more and be healthier for having participated in them.

Of course, whether it is healthy habits or being loved, or mental development, one of the most important aspects of loving our children is to set a good example for them.

Children watch everything. They are great at picking up contradictions between what we say and what we do as parents. Someone once said that one of the best gifts a man can give his children is to love their mother. I am sure the same can be said as far as a mother loving the father. What that comment means is that children learn about love not only from how they are treated, but also from how their parents love each other. Children see and notice everything. They may not fully understand what they see, but they internalize and eventually mirror the type of adult relationships they see in their parents. They take that relationship to be the norm. For children to see and experience the love between the two most important adults in their lives is one of the most wonderful gifts parents can give their children. I know that some parents don't always love each other in the way that they should or would like to. But if it is important to an adult to raise strong and capable children into human beings who can be happy in the deepest sense of the term, the adult needs to think about what example they are setting for their children when it comes to how they relate to the other parent.

Love does not mean giving our children everything they want. First of all, most things that most of us want are desires created by outside influences. In today's world, most of those desires are created by a never-ending and constant barrage of advertising. Parents need to provide a reasonable amount of material things to our children so that they can function effectively and comfortably in the environment in which the children live. But providing them with everything they think they need is not good for children.

As children get older, the ways we express love to our children change. Physical affection is still important. But as children grow and develop, they begin to see and understand themselves as distinct individuals. They are still part of the family, but are also separate and unique persons. One of the most important ways that we show our love to our children as they grow into this unique person is to treat them with respect as an individual with all of the qualities and capabilities they are and have at each particular stage of their development.

Respect Our Children

Respect children as individual human beings who are as worthy of respect and attention as we think ourselves to be. We should not impose our own will and expectations on our children in an arbitrary manner. As parents, it is our job to guide and train our children so that they grow up to be good people. And, in the process of growing up, it is our job as parents to see that they do not do something which will seriously injure themselves or others. But we must always keep in mind that they are distinct individuals and human beings who are worthy of the same type of respectful interaction which we would accord to another adult.

Respect means not imposing our fantasies onto our children's lives. Wanting a child to be a Super Bowl quarterback or Olympic gold medal winner is often more of a reflection of what the parent wants than what the child wants. Certainly, if a child has unusual talent, it should be fostered as best the parents can do and afford. But children can grow up and be happy and full human beings without an Olympic medal or Super Bowl ring.

Similarly, the schools that children go to do not have to be the most prestigious schools. Parents who fight to get their children into the "best" schools are doing so to meet their own ambitions and fantasies. Children can grow up to be productive and wonderfully talented people without going to Yale or Harvard. Certainly such schools put children in contact with people and institutions which can help them succeed.   But most great artists, athletes, business leaders, and scientists come from schools all over the country and all over the world. Giving our children a love of learning is more important than what schools they go to.

Let children be children. Let them play. Let them enjoy the carefree aspects of childhood while they have the opportunity to do so. Play fosters the growth of imagination and creativity in children which they carry into adulthood. Scheduling every minute of every day is not necessary or good for children.

Again, the role that we play as parents with our children is different than the role we have with another adult. And that role and relationship will change as children get older. As children grow and develop, children know more and become more capable of making decisions that affect their well-being. Parents have to be aware of that growth and development in their children and change their own role in relationship to the children as the relationship moves toward equality as human beings between the children and the parents.

We must always keep in mind that our children are separate persons and it is our job to see that that distinct individual child grows and flourishes into what she or he, as an individual human being, can and should be. And we need to recognize that what the individual child is and can be is different than what we may want them to be. Importantly, we should not expect one of our children to be the same as any of our other children.

Respecting our children means that we listen to them and try to comprehend their understanding of reality.   Respect means that we do not belittle them or make derogatory remarks to them or about them. Respect means that we treat them appropriately for their age. We should not treat a ten-year-old the same way we treat a five-year-old, a seven-year-old, or a fifteen-year-old.

Sometimes, as parents, we must exercise authority. That is our job and responsibility. But respectfully exercising authority means that discussion, reason, love (care and concern for their well-being), and respect should be the guidelines and practices within which we approach and impose discipline.

Physical coercion and inflicting physical pain on our children should hardly ever be used. And if it is used, it should be done in a calculating manner to emphasize the importance of certain behaviors and not as a manifestation of our out-of-control anger. One of the few circumstances which justify some physical force being applied to a child is when a young child runs out on a street. Certainly, talking with the child about the danger of being run over by a car may have an effect on the child's behavior. But with a two-year-old, reason and rationality is in short supply. If the child runs into the street a second time, then a couple of firm whacks on the rear-end will get the child's attention, particularly if that is the first, and maybe only, time that physical punishment has been used by the parent.

Finally, when it comes to disciplining our children, it is important to understand that the word discipline is derived from the word disciple, which in turn is related to the words teacher and follower. Discipline administered by a parent should above all be an opportunity to teach. Discipline should be built around intelligent and open discussion befitting the age and maturity of the child. Punishments like "grounding" or similar withholding of access to things that children like or want have some value in terms of possibly making the children think about the negative consequences of their actions. But such punishments seldom have the desired effect because there is usually no teaching, learning and growth in understanding taking place.

Like everything else, approaching discipline as a teaching and learning opportunity for both children and parents takes time. And by taking that time to discuss unacceptable behaviors, children can learn about and understand the rationale and values behind desired behaviors. At the same time, parents can learn about where the children are in their intellectual and emotional development and about the world that the children live in. It is much easier to ground or otherwise punish a child than to discuss with them the pros and cons of different behaviors as well as why they might not want to behave in a way which the parent thinks might bring harm to the child or to others.

Give Children the Time They Need

Nothing shows any person, adult or child, that they are loved and respected as giving that person individualized time and attention.

Everything in life takes time. We allocate our time based on our priorities. If the growth and development of our children along the lines described earlier in this chapter is a high priority for us, then we must devote time to being in relationship with our children throughout their lives.

How we spend time with our children depends on their stage of development. The following suggestions are not intended to be comprehensive and touch on every stage of a child's development. Hopefully, however, they will illustrate two things: first, that as the child grows, they need different types of interaction from their parent; and, two, that most of the things we can do with our child to show that we love and respect them are relatively simple and inexpensive. But they do cost time and attention to who the individual child is and what fits her or him.

Nothing is more important during the first year or two of a child's life than to hold and hug the child often. Children learn in their basic wiring that they are loved and cared for simply because they exist.

As they go through their pre-school years, reading and playing with and/or engaging in physical activities with our children are new ways in which to spend time with them. These years begin with the "terrible twos" when our children begin to recognize themselves as individuals and as separate entities from their parents and their environment. They are also years when our children's curiosity and hunger for knowledge is exploding. Engaging in activities with our children which feed that hunger is a good way to spend time with them.

Distraction and re-direction of children's focus and energies is better than confrontation with small children. Children are very focused. It is hard to have a stronger will than a child. As a parent, we have many things we are dealing with as far as being a parent, a spouse, a worker, a community member, etc. Young children are usually single-mindedly focused on what is in front of them and what they want. Adults will lose most battles of wills unless the parent resorts to physical punishment. If the parent does resort to physical punishment, they may win the battle, but they will lose the war as far as having a loving and respectful relationship which grows through life.

As they enter school and a more formal learning environment, children still need support in learning. They also move into a different social environment. Spend time talking with them about their academic and social experiences in school. As their physical coordination, skills, and capacities grow, be involved with them in developing those skills and abilities. Play sports with them. Go walking or biking with them. And do those activities with them for the fun of it and so that they learn that being physically active and developing whatever physical skills they have is enjoyable and satisfying in and of itself.

As they progress through elementary school, children continue to learn, they become more involved socially, and the begin seeing themselves as more distinct individuals. Again, talking with your children about their experiences is very important. During this time period, parents need to be more aware of and careful about being too judgmental about what the child thinks. Fortunately, as the child grows into and through this stage of their life, they do become more knowledgeable. As parents, the discussions we have with our children should reflect this developing self-knowledge and budding sense of uniqueness and individuality.

Then, of course, there are the teen years when the quest for individuality and separateness from the parents and their values drives parents crazy. Conversation needs to continue, but again, at a different level of appreciation by the parent of the developmental events and changes in the growing child's life. And though teenagers want to be more and more on their own, they still want to interact with the parents and other family members. One of the jobs of the parent at this stage of development is to figure out what kinds of activity their children want to still engage in with their parents.

Throughout all of these stages of growth and development, one other challenge to being a good parent is to balance giving direction to the child with giving them the room to develop the autonomy they desire and need to be a good human being.

If we bring children into this world, it is our responsibility to see that we help them grow and develop into good human beings. That doesn't just happen. It takes knowledge, time, and effort, which we will only give to our children if we know what we are aiming for in raising them and if doing so is a high priority for us as parents.

There is no specific roadmap on what to do in every circumstance that arises during the growth and development of the child.

But if we as parents love our children, treat them with respect, and give them the time they need and deserve, then we will make mostly correct decisions in raising them. None of us will raise our children perfectly. But we can raise them either for better or worse, depending on how close we come to what we want our children to really be:

A *developing human person who flourishes as*
-a unique combination of body and spirit,
-who exists in relationship to other things and people, and
-who has the capacity of:
- *Learning and knowing.*
- *Self-awareness, subjective knowledge, self-consciousness.*
- *Imagination and creativity.*
- *Evaluating and choosing.*
- *Loving and being loved.*

CHAPTER TWENTY-SIX

Have Fun!

Having fun seems like a strange chapter to have in a book which addresses serious and profound questions and issues. But having fun is one of the keys to being a flourishing human being and living a happy and good life. Taking life seriously does not mean that we have to live our life with a frown and without pleasure, enjoyment, and enthusiasm. In fact, I think if we take life seriously and try to understand who and what we are as human beings as well as all of the realities around us as best we can, the opportunities for having fun and enjoying our lives increase substantially.

We live in a wondrous world that is full of beauty, people and things to know, and activities to participate in and enjoy. We too often forget that as we grow older. We get bogged down with work and the other difficulties and challenges of life. We miss out on real fun, enjoyment, and recreation which most accurately should be looked at as re-creation: i.e., the rejuvenation and renewal of ourselves through leisure time activities which help us develop the more playful and fun aspects of who we are as human beings.

Also, life is very frantic today. It has become more so over the last 40 years. The pressures to work and acquire have become two of the main motivators for many of us. Also, constant stimulation by media of all kinds makes it difficult for us to slow down and be in touch with whom we really are as well as the realities (including other people) outside of ourselves. Instant gratification is available to most of us most of the time. Consequently, we end up accepting the instant gratification (ingesting quantities of junk food, watching too much TV, cell phone calls, text messaging, video games, etc., etc.) and the related physical stimulation related to those activities (sugar highs, quasi-emotional highs from seeing our favorite team win, being "wired" in every sense of that word) over the long-term flourishing of ourselves and the rest of reality. Attention deficit disorder is a growing phenomenon among children and adults. Certainly some individuals have some real cognitive deficits regarding how their brain works. But frankly, the growing numbers of attention deficit disorder diagnoses are more the result of sugar and caffeine laced diets and a constant barrage of short and attention-grabbing video and sound messages which bombard all of us constantly than any mental incapacity.

Though it is hard to define the word "fun," I think it is instructive and a good reminder about how to approach having fun by observing children. They are fascinated by so much around them. They focus their attention so strongly and intently on everything they encounter as they learn about themselves and the rest of reality. They are totally open to what they encounter. They are not stressed out while they do this. It comes naturally to them. It is what they do as human beings. They learn constantly. And, though young children cannot articulate their joy in learning, we can see it in their faces. Children who are learning are happy.

Watch young children play by themselves. Again, they are totally engaged with their activities. They use their imaginations and are creative in their play. They try new things when they play. They see what works and doesn't work. They use their bodies to move and they enjoy the movement for its own sake. Watch children learn to crawl and walk. They are delighted when they do so because physical movement is part of what it means to be human and one of the joys of life is to move, particularly if we are able to do it gracefully and/or athletically.

As we grow older, learning can often become a chore and not a delight. Learning becomes something we do in order to get good grades, or get into a better school, or get a better job, or keep our jobs. All of those are reasonable goals, but too often the practicalities of life drive out the sheer joy of learning. And the joy of learning is something we should always try to keep as part of our lives. We can do that only if we are aware that learning can and should be fun in and of itself, and then consciously make decisions and choices to pursue those learning experiences.

We can learn from an intellectual and practical standpoint. From an intellectual standpoint, we can learn by reading, listening to and engaging in conversation with other people, particularly people who are learned in their field of interest, and by experiencing the realities of topics from anthropology to zoology.

From a practical standpoint, we can learn to do things with our hands and other physical attributes we possess. We can learn about a wide range of arts and crafts. We can learn how to engage in those activities so that we can perform them in a manner which can produce something useful and/or beautiful. We can also engage in a wide variety of physical activities which enlarge our experience and give us opportunities to develop our physical talents and skills. Two common avenues of such learning and experience are sports and music-related activities such as dancing and playing a musical instrument. Human beings initially participate in these physical activities for the sheer joy of it. Sports combine physical movement and play, two aspects of us as human beings which constitute who we are and what we enjoy doing.

The examples above just touch on the vast variety of intellectual and physical activities which we can engage in as human beings for the fun of it. There are many, many more which fit all of us differently based on the particular talents, skills, and interests we possess. There are also a wide variety of fun things to do mentally and physically which can be done on a solitary basis or on a more social and interactive basis.

One important thing about having fun is to generally be proactively engaged with realities inside and outside of ourselves. Occasionally, passive entertainment can be fun and enjoyable and good for us, particularly if we are tired and need a physical and/or mental and psychological break. In today's world, television and related communications media are readily available almost non-stop whether we want to be exposed to such media or not. Studies have consistently shown that watching TV for people of any age is basically a passive activity which deadens our minds, shortens our attention spans, and has negative physical impacts. The term and picture of a typical "couch potato" is not far off from reality. Certainly there are occasionally programs of value on television which can inform us and entertain us. But most TV fare is pure drivel and adds little if anything to our enjoyment of life and our growth, development, and flourishing as human beings. TV way too often steals our time and seldom leaves us really feeling joyful.

Also, being a sports spectator should be allowed a limited amount of our time, particularly as it is televised. Observing the athleticism and talents of individual athletes and teams is enjoyable and sometimes even inspiring. When done in a group setting, as it often is, it can be an enjoyable social event and build a certain amount of camaraderie among spectators whether at the sports venue or on TV. The stories and statistics related to sports can be enjoyable topics of learning and discussion. But watching sports is not as beneficial to our well-being and flourishing as participating in them or other physical activities. I think one of the things that has been lost in the over-emphasis of spectator sports is the sheer joy of playing games which inspired human beings to invent games of various types over the years.

Playing at anything (physical or mental) at any age is good for us as human beings. Playing at anything should be mentally relaxing, as it removes us from the daily grind of reality and calls on our creative and imaginative powers. Unfortunately, the sheer joy of play has been squeezed out of many sports, starting at the earliest competitive levels. Professional teams scout college athletes, colleges scout high school athletes, and high schools are starting to scout and recruit elementary school athletes with greater frequency. Athletes at all levels down to elementary schools are expected to pursue their sport year round with special training, camps, and programs which will give them a better shot at succeeding at their area of specialty. The emphasis is on winning, which is okay up to a point. But the real emphasis should be on the joy of playing and competing. Too often those elements of sports are minimized or totally negated by the unfortunate over-emphasis on sports. Adults have imposed their concept and emphasis on winning on sports at all levels and for all ages of athletes. All too often, adults have taken away from children the enjoyment, creativity, and non-judgmental aspects of playing sports. Today, kids always seem to be in uniform and they are always accompanied by adults who are coaching them. I think that is a real and significant loss to human flourishing.

Like just about everything in life, we need a balance between active and passive recreation, between physical and mental pursuits, between solitary and social/team activities. That balance is different for all of us. Part of living a good and happy life, and flourishing as a human being, is to think about and find a mix of fun activities and pursuits which fit who and what we are as individuals and social beings. Too often, we all get pulled into a set of non-work activities which are supposed to make us happy, but don't do so. None of us can control that entirely. But if we never think about what types of non-work activities would make us happy and flourish, we will be missing out on another opportunity to live a full and happy life.

CHAPTER TWENTY-SEVEN

Uncertainty

I think one of the hardest things about living a good life…a happy life…a life that is fitting and proper for a human being, is that we are seldom absolutely certain of what it takes to do that.

I have just written a number of chapters which point to what I think are good ways to lead our lives happily and as flourishing human beings. I think there are a lot of good principles and general guidelines contained in those chapters. But like everyone else, when it comes time to make a decision about any important and concrete matter which will affect my happiness or the happiness of those I love, I experience uncertainty, too.

I think I have minimized some of the uncertainty for myself in my life by utilizing the ideas and principles set forth previously. But I am not certain how those general principles and mindset apply to any and every particular/concrete situation which I will encounter as a separate individual or as part of a group.

Consequently, I think it is worth some time to exam the idea of uncertainty.

What is uncertainty?

- <u>A feeling</u> - It is an emotional response which may or may not be valid.
- <u>Of fear and anxiety</u> - Both emotions are unpleasant. We want to eliminate them.
- <u>Which we experience when we are not sure what to do</u> - See the reasons listed below.

- <u>Based on our perception that our well-being is threatened</u> - In a real life/non-theoretical situation.
- <u>If we don't act in a way that protects our well-being.</u> - We must decide/choose a course of action.

We experience that same feeling when the well-being of people we know and love is also threatened.

Why do we experience uncertainty and how do we cope with it?

Why Do We Experience Uncertainty?

We experience uncertainty for four main reasons:

- Reality is extremely complex.
- The future is unpredictable.
- Anxiety is part of the human makeup.
- Our understanding of what is necessary for happiness is often not clear.

<u>Reality is extremely complex.</u> Though we try to simplify things as much as we can, we seldom comprehend the broad range of realities which confront us, particularly where human beings and human interactions are concerned. It is hard enough to understand the physical make up of material things such as an atom, a plant, a building, a car, or anything that we interact with daily. And even though we understand more and more about material reality through science and practical experience, there are still huge gaps and unanswered questions that the best scientific minds still grapple with and about which we non-scientists understand even less. When emotional, psychological, and spiritual factors enter into the picture, as well as elements of history and time, knowing everything we need to

know before making a decision which will protect or advance our well-being and the well-being of those we love is pretty near impossible. It is safe to say that in almost every important situation in our lives, we never know enough to be certain of the outcome. Hence, we feel uncertain.

The future is unpredictable. There are so many variables affecting most of reality that we are unable to predict how decisions on our part will be affected by them. First of all, there is just pure, "dumb luck." Cars cross medians and hit other cars head-on and kill all of the occupants. People go to work and someone flies a plane into their office building and thousands die. Students go to class and some deranged person decides to shoot everyone they see. Someone buys a lottery ticket and actually wins the big prize. All of us have good luck and bad luck. We can't control our luck. We can do things to minimize our exposure to bad luck and maximize our opportunities so we might capitalize on good luck. But we really can't control luck. So we experience uncertainty.

Also, there are huge social, cultural, political, and economic forces which impact all of us, sometimes for good and sometimes for ill. These forces are sometimes thought of as good luck and bad luck. Certainly losing a job or a home because of a bad economy can be considered bad luck to the ones losing those things. But in reality, the changes in these huge forces are usually the result of decisions made by people with power who try to shape these forces to meet what they perceive as their well-being or fitting into some broad ideology. However, even then, those who try to shape these forces seldom understand the huge complexities and multiple variables affecting the outcomes of what they are trying to achieve. So all of us are subject to these changes and we do not know how they will affect us.

Finally, human beings are very unpredictable. Our knowledge about ourselves is ever evolving and never complete. Our knowledge of other human beings is even less complete. It is impossible to answer with certainty questions such as: "Who should I marry?" Or, "How will my children turn out?" Or "What career fits me?" Even less complicated and shorter range questions concerning many everyday situations we encounter interacting with people at work, at school, at home, and in our community have many variables that we do not know or understand. So, again, we experience uncertainty.

<u>Anxiety is part of the human makeup.</u> We are all familiar with the "fight or flight" reaction that we as human beings experience when confronted with threats to our well-being and the well-being of those we love. It is a natural, self-preservation instinct and behavior that we all possess. Whether we chose to fight or flee when we are confronted with a threat, we are uncertain of the outcome and we experience the emotions of fear and anxiety. The deepest fear of most people is that their human life will end sooner rather than later. For many, it is not only a fear of the loss of their human life, but also of their existence. They fear that once they die, they will no longer exist as anything. That uncertainty about our ultimate existence causes human beings to be uncertain about the future at the deepest core of who and what we are. Consequently, there is an underlying emotional sense of uncertainty and anxiety which affects all human beings.

<u>Our understanding of what is necessary for happiness is often not clear.</u> Most of us do not know ourselves as well as we should or could. Consequently, we don't know what will really make us happy. We too easily accept what others tell us will make us happy. Usually, those telling us what will make us happy have self-serving motives whether they are advertisers, cultural/economic/political leaders,

and/or religious institutions. One reason we are uncertain about what will make us truly happy is because if and when we attain one of the things that we are told will make us happy, and the happiness we experience is fleeting, or non-existent, or is actually bad for us, we get confused. We become more uncertain about what we should be choosing to do, or to buy, or to be in order to be happy because we are told one thing, but the reality of the experience does not live up to the hype.

How Do We Cope With Uncertainty?

How we cope with uncertainty is very important to our happiness and well-being, and the happiness and well-being of those we love and of the rest of reality with which we interact.

I think there are three main strategies that most people adopt to deal with uncertainty:

- We distract ourselves so as not to experience the unpleasant emotions connected to uncertainty.
- We try to learn as much as possible.
- We develop a basic mindset which helps us make decisions.

<u>We distract ourselves so as not to experience the unpleasant emotions connected to uncertainty.</u> An all too frequent and easy approach to dealing with uncertainty is to distract ourselves from dealing with the underlying anxiety and fear which we all experience. The distractions are easy to come by in the modern world. There is a never-ending stream of stimuli to which we are all subject whether or not we want to be exposed to such distraction. We cannot escape attempts to sell us something which we are told will make us happy and make us feel good about ourselves. Many people are addicted to

stimulation of one kind or another. Some people use a variety of substances to distract themselves from the underlying anxiety and fear that they experience. Drugs (illegal and prescriptions), alcohol, highly-caffeinated drinks, and sugar-laced foods are among the many stimulants which mask our feelings. Constant work is another escape from our feelings of uncertainty. Serial sexual relationships are another distraction that some people pursue. There is no end to the kinds of distractions which we are subject to or which we can actively pursue.

On the other hand, it takes a conscious choice and decision to not constantly be subject to such stimuli and distractions. Most of us are not taught that we should avoid the constant stimulation. We just take it as part of the reality in which we live. The constant stimulation and distraction is not good for our physical, emotional, or spiritual health and well-being. It temporarily buries the anxiety and fear associated with uncertainty, but it takes a toll on who and what we are and can be as flourishing human beings.

<u>We try to learn as much as possible</u>. Most of us seem to do pretty well learning the practical things we need to know for our jobs and our everyday living. Depending on the nature of our jobs, we may always need to learn new things in order to perform satisfactorily and continue to make a living. The more we learn in these areas, the less uncertainty we experience in handling those aspects of our lives.

Unfortunately, many of us do not learn as much as we can about the less practical but also very important aspects of reality, particularly who and what we are as human beings and what we should be aiming for in order to be happy and flourishing as human beings. Some people pick up a self-improvement book now and then. Others watch television gurus such as Oprah and Dr. Phil to learn about some of the areas which we need to know about in order to be developing human beings. All of these brief attempts to learn have some value. But most of them are very superficial. They do not ask or attempt to answer some of the deepest questions about reality and how we as human beings fit into that reality in a positive and appropriate manner.

For most of us, most of the time, we learn how to act and make decisions based on examples of what others do or tell us to do in order to be happy. As we are growing up, we learn from our parents and other adults in our lives. As we get older, we learn from our friends. In our celebrity-crazed western world, we follow the example of "stars" of any type (music, films, TV, sports) regarding what we should pursue and try to attain or obtain to be happy. Learning from example is good if we are learning from good examples which show us how to live as true and full human beings. On the other hand, learning about what is important in life from a movie star is, in most cases, not going to be helpful to us, make us happy, or make us more of what a human being can and should be.

We develop a basic mindset which helps us make decisions. Since it is not only difficult but impossible to know everything we need to know about everything in order to make good decisions which we are certain will promote our flourishing as human beings, as well as the flourishing of others, we all adopt one or more mindsets which help us make decisions on a timely basis as they need to be made.

For most people, this mindset is composed of several elements. There is usually a component that is picked up from our families as we are growing up. There is often a religious element for many people. Our formal education contributes to the development of our overall mindset. So do our jobs and our social interactions with people from our family, work, and community. Our own experience is a big contributor to our mindset. And, very importantly, there are the examples that we see lived out by others which we see as sometimes leading to a successful and happy conclusion to a choice that is made and other times leading to disasters.

Most of us adopt a mix of ideas and beliefs which guide our actions with a reasonable amount of certainty as to the outcome. The mix of ideas and beliefs allows us flexibility in addressing life's important issues based on the specifics of the situations which we encounter. The mix of ideas allows us to see reality more clearly and completely, and then to respond accordingly.

Some people, on the other hand, adopt a very specific and comprehensive set of ideas and/or beliefs and live by them. Such comprehensive mindsets (e.g., communism, socialism, democracy, capitalism, Catholicism, Islam, Evangelicalism, Darwinism, scientific reductionism, etc.) usually have an answer for every question and a prescribed course of action to take in every circumstance. Whether the mindset is intellectually or religiously based, the "ism" that such people adopt may speak to some issues well and may provide a solid grounding for making some decisions and choices with certainty. There really are some good things about most "isms." But no "ism" is comprehensive enough to speak to all aspects of reality, no matter how much the proponents of the "ism" claim it to be so.

In instances where the "ism" is the basis for making all decisions, certainty is achieved, but responding to the true reality of each specific circumstance is lost. It is a trade-off many people make. They often make the trade off without realizing they are doing so. In their minds, feeling anxious and fearful is very uncomfortable for them. The certainty related to an "ism' removes that anxiety and fear. Interestingly, there is a related, internal element of uncertainty associated with every "ism." That is the uncertainty that the person who adheres to an "ism" is not doing so completely and correctly. If they do not adhere to the dictates of the "ism," they often feel guilty, fearful and/or anxious that they will be condemned to hell or ostracized from a political party or movement, or even killed by the party or movement if they do not toe the line completely and correctly. The only way to assure certainty then is to adopt the "ism" wholly and completely and make it apply to every decision and choice they make. Another aspect of adopting an "ism" totally and completely is that it leads some individuals and groups to attack people and organizations which threaten their world view. Sometimes the attacks are verbal and sometimes they are physical. Some people become hateful towards others who do not share their viewpoint. The hate is harmful to others, but also harms the people who are filled with hate by corroding and harming their own lives spiritually, mentally, emotionally, and physically.

On the other hand, being open to discerning the reality of things and situations can be scary. It does produce some anxiety and fear. But it has the great plus of allowing us to live in closer relationship to true reality in all of its complexity and variety. It also takes more time sometimes to understand a situation. It requires us to consciously form a mindset by devoting time to reading and thinking about who and what we are and what we are encountering outside of ourselves. It takes time and effort to interact with reality on an intellectual and spiritual basis. But the ultimate trade-off for this time and effort is an overall better set of decisions and choices which allow us and the realities outside of ourselves to flourish as we and those realities can and should.

Summary

I like to look at certainty on a continuum, just like I did with knowledge and belief. I try to be at the higher end of the certainty continuum (maybe 75% or better on the scale), but I know that I won't always be there. In fact, I think all of us are seldom there if we are truly open to reality and are not trying to fit it into our preconceived ideas, beliefs, and/or opinions.

Continuum of Certainty

0%		100%
Certainty	————————————————————	Certainty

Our certainty when it comes to making a decision can be anywhere along the line depending on our knowledge and credible belief. A goal of 100% certainty, though it seems desirable, is not always possible or even desirable to attain. For example, if I feel 100% certain about a decision I plan to make (marry a certain person), but the decision turns out to have negative consequences for myself and the other person (we find out that we have very different ideas about having a child or children), then being 100% certain beforehand was not a plus. In fact, if I was a little more uncertain about the success of the marriage, maybe I would have discussed both of our ideas regarding children before the marriage and we would have avoided a painful time for both of us.

On the other hand, I may not be 100% certain that I should marry a certain person. Maybe I am 50-50 on the matter. However, after thoughtfully thinking through some of my concerns and doubts, and discussing them with the person I intend to marry, maybe my sense of certainty increases to a 70% to 30% ratio. And, in fact, even with, or maybe because of that uncertainty, we end up having a long and happy marriage because we regularly discussed the important elements of our life together and made decisions which were mutually beneficial to each of us and our long-term relationship.

We will never remove uncertainty and its related feelings of fear and anxiety from our lives entirely. But we can do several things that will help us deal with uncertainty more successfully and which will allow us to make better decisions and choices relative to our own well-being and the well-being of realities outside of ourselves:

1. Accept the fact that uncertainty is part of the human condition. We will never be absolutely certain of most things.

2. Do not run from or try to hide from the negative and uncomfortable feelings that uncertainty engenders. They are a natural part of life. They push us towards greater understanding so that we can protect ourselves from harm and lead us to grow and flourish as human beings.

3. Be open to reality. Try to understand reality as it truly is, not as we prejudge it to be or want it to be. Be a lifelong learner regarding all aspects of reality including both the practical/material and the spiritual.

4. Be careful of "isms" of any kind. Some have more value and have lasted longer than others because they are more reflective of reality. But no "ism" has the answer to every one of life's problems and challenges.

5. Don't give up the pursuit of understanding reality in exchange for getting rid of the negative feelings of fear and anxiety associated with uncertainty.

6. Evaluate situations and make decisions based on what promotes the well-being of ourselves, others, and the broader world in which we live.

7. Be quiet sometimes. Be still. Learn to be comfortable with our thoughts and with silence.

8. Consciously develop a mindset that is well grounded in the reality of who and what we are as human beings:

Human persons in time who are unique combinations of body and spirit, with particular histories, who exist in relationship to other things and people, and who have the capacity of: learning and knowing; self-awareness, subjective knowledge, and self-consciousness; imagination and creativity; evaluating and choosing; loving and being loved; dying and knowing we will die.

And the last two things to remember and think about, at least for me as a person who makes choices and decisions based on knowledge and credible belief:

1. Pray for wisdom, the combination of broad-based knowledge and loving care and consideration (head and heart), to help us make decisions and take action which will lead to the best possible outcomes.

2. Consciously develop a mindset that has as an important element the credible belief that no matter what good or evil we experience in our lives and the lives of those we love, including death, we will continue to exist, flourish, and be happy in an existence which is changed but not ended.

CHAPTER TWENTY-EIGHT

Summary and Conclusion

Read, listen, observe, and think in order to learn and understand as much of reality as we can.

Seek out, develop, and nurture loving relationships with other human beings.

Pursuing both of these uniquely human capacities and abilities will assist us in making choices and decisions which will contribute to our happiness and flourishing as human beings.

But, we are not only knowing and loving beings. We have bodies. We need to take care of them as well. Our bodies bring us pleasure and happiness, and those good things that please our senses of sight, sound, smell, touch and taste should also be pursued. The only caveat is that, as good as those things are, they need to be pursued within the broader framework of what and who we are as human beings, which means they need to be pursued intelligently, moderately, and responsibly. And, they need to be pursued in the context of how they help us know and love as only human beings are capable of doing.

Have courage! It is not easy to live a life which so often butts up against what popular culture considers the pursuit of happiness to be. It is not that everything about popular culture at any time of history, including now, is hurtful to us as human beings. There are many good things which we can and should pursue within our culture and have fun doing so. But don't be misled that obtaining or achieving some of the goals presented to us by our culture as happiness producing will lead us to as full and true a happiness as pursuing those activities which make us uniquely human.

Have courage also, because it is not easy living life the way that fits us best as human beings. None of us really knows what that is all of the time under different circumstances and in different situations. But if we have a solid base of understanding of what and who we are as human beings, we will make more happiness producing decisions than not over our lifetime.

I like to look at our understanding of ourselves as human beings as the basic foundation of a happy and good life. Maybe it is because I have built a number of things over the years. Consequently, the concept of having a strong foundation as essential to building something well and something which will last has always appealed to me. The stronger the foundation, the chances are better that the buildings, the relationships, the projects and programs, the businesses, the sports, and anything else I pursue, will flourish.

Greatness in any area of life is usually built on a strong foundation of knowledge and skills that are appropriate to the activity. Great artists learn the basics of the artistic techniques necessary for accomplishing their artistic endeavors. Great athletes learn the basics of their sport necessary to accomplish their athletic endeavors. It is the same in every aspect of life. The great artists, athletes, and successes at any human endeavor learn their craft. And once they know, understand and practice the basics of their craft, they can then bring their own unique talents and gifts to create a true work of art, or a truly awe-inspiring athletic achievement, or a memorable and successful achievement in any area of life.

That is why I also like to look at living life as a lifetime artistic endeavor. If we understand the basics of what and who we are as a human being, we will then be able to build a life which brings our own unique talents, abilities, and sensibilities to each situation we meet in life. We can create a life which is a work of art. A life in which we enjoy ourselves. And also a life which is beautiful and good, and often inspiring to those around us.

We can and should live at the highest level that human beings are capable of doing. We are wonderful and wondrous beings engaged in and with an unbelievably beautiful and meaningful world.

We can be part of co-creating and re-creating the world if we choose to do so.

We are called to be good and happy human beings.

It is never too late in life to pursue that goal.

I think the ideas that have been set forth in this book can help us do so.